UNION TERROR

UNION TERROR

DEBUNKING THE FALSE JUSTIFICATIONS FOR UNION TERROR AGAINST SOUTHERN CIVILIANS IN THE AMERICAN CIVIL WAR

DR. JEFFREY F. ADDICOTT

LT. COLONEL (US ARMY, RET.) BA, JD, LLM (2), SJD

This book is dedicated to the courage, spirit,
and sacrifice of my parents:

CDR Leslie Addicott, Jr., (U.S. Navy, Ret.)

&

Mrs. Eloise Addicott

Produced in the Republic of South Carolina by
SHOTWELL PUBLISHING LLC
Post Office Box 2592
Columbia, So. Carolina 29202
www.ShotwellPublishing.com

Cover Design: Boo Jackson. Portrait public domain courtesy of Library Of Congress. All other design elements CC0.

ISBN: 978-1-947660-82-3

FIRST EDITION

10 9 8 7 6 5 4 3 2 1

Contents

INTRODUCTION

*The trouble with man is twofold – he cannot learn
truths that are too complicated and he forgets truths
that are too simple.[1]*   *– Rebecca West*

THE WAR BETWEEN THE STATES, more popularly known as the
Civil War, lasted for four long years and soaked the ground red
with the lifeblood of its people. Not only was it the most significant
event in American history, but the Northern victory inaugurated
a more closely shared national identity of "Americanism," while
simultaneously providing the fledgling democracy with a long
overdue course-correction – the repulsive institution of human
bondage was finally abolished. While the War was not solely
about slavery, the War ended slavery. Indeed, out of the ashes of
an internal firestorm that claimed the lives of well over 750,000
people,[2] the country moved significantly closer to Thomas
Jefferson's aspirational vision of the God-given rights of "life,
liberty, and the pursuit of happiness" for all of its inhabitants.

Fully confident that a merciful and providential God controlled
the wheels of history Robert E. Lee, the South's greatest son, rejoiced
over this profound and positive outcome. With the War lost, the
South ravaged, and finding himself in personal poverty, Lee was
nevertheless able to point with abiding satisfaction to the abolition
of slavery as the preeminent positive for the Southern people. In
May 1870, just five months before his death in Lexington, Virginia,
Lee voiced this truth:

> So far from engaging in a war to perpetuate slavery, I
> am rejoiced that slavery is abolished. I believe it will
> be greatly for the interest of the South. So fully am I
> satisfied of this ... that I would cheerfully have lost all
> I have lost by the war and suffered all I have suffered,
> to have this object attained.[3]

— Rejecting Terrorism —

There are, of course, many other core positives that can be gleaned from the Civil War, not the least of which is the stark reminder that command directed barbarism against civilian noncombatants can never be justified. As clearly seen with Russia's 2022 invasion of Ukraine, both basic humanity and the law of war — then and now — absolutely prohibit soldiers from terrorizing the innocents of the opposing country with depredations. Regardless of all "end justifies the means" rants to excuse wartime atrocities, the necessity for civilized nations to abide by the long recognized legal and moral *jus ad bellum* requirements of the law of armed conflict can never be abrogated. Tragically, as this book will reveal, the Union military hierarchy intentionally engaged in the vile practice of terror on innocent civilians, inflicting unnecessary pain and suffering on a massive scale.

While the Union generally abided by the law of war in the first two years of its invasion of the Confederacy, the Lincoln Administration became exasperated with its lack of military success to win the war and by 1864 cold-heartedly adopted a despicable new strategy to subjugate the South. To students of history, the new strategy was really nothing new — it was the infliction of raw terror against the civilian population. In short, war crimes were committed on an unprecedented scale.

Strangely, although this important lesson finds its discussion centered primarily on the victor's wanton use of terror against Southern civilians, it has long been swept under the rug as a *verboten* subject of scholarship and discussion. With few exceptions, when it comes to addressing the Union's use of terrorism, America's story books are stone silent. As they say, the winners write the history books. Nevertheless, given that the Civil War is the most studied conflict in American history, it is rather striking that the topic of Union terrorism against Southern civilians is seldom mentioned in the voluminous literature other than as a cursory aside or footnote. While some might place the blame for this paucity of discussion on the fact that the topic itself runs counter to the general reputation of the American soldier as an ethical war fighter, the more likely explanation rests in the sad phenomenon that to admit or even to explore the viciousness of Union wrongdoing might be interpreted as somehow showing sympathy to the Confederacy or to the South, an academic a position that is absolutely anathema, particularly in this age of historical revisionism. Without question, the new group-think trends of "reimagining" American history which has infected the culture dictates what we are allowed to say out loud or pen in writing. This is so much so that Americans are required to flatly deny any aspect of our national heritage that fails to conform to the machinations of the cancel culture or be subjected to great social opprobrium if they don't.

The result of such intellectual bankruptcy is tragic. Like a gigantic ice-berg the real truth about Union sponsored terrorism in the Civil War is almost entirely submerged below the surface of the fact-free viewpoint of "presentism," defined as "an uncritical adherence to present-day attitudes, especially the tendency to interpret past events in terms of modern values and concepts."[4] Historical illiterates and ideologues have led the gullible into simplistic cul-de-sacs of the make believe or "fake history," and if ever challenged with incontrovertible hard evidence about the horrors of Union atrocities, the emotional retort is generally coated with sophomoric and wrongheaded platitudes about how the end, defeating the South, justified the means, conducting an intentional policy of raw terror on Southern civilians.

– Dispelling the Justifications for Terror –

Rubricated by William T. Sherman as the chief purveyor of atrocities, with his pillaging campaigns in Mississippi, Georgia and South Carolina, Lincoln allowed his generals to employ a scorched-earth policy of terror aimed directly at the innocent women, children, and elderly of the South. Casting aside all civilized and binding legal norms – even the ones Lincoln himself codified for his soldiers as General Order 100 in April 1863 – the United States disgraced itself by stooping to the *chevauhee*, where medieval European militaries on the move would systematically pillage and burn out everything and everyone in their path of march.

While the facts in this regard are unambiguous, there are many who shield the Union's use of terror with a variety of empty-headed "justifications," to include the "end justifies the means" contention mentioned above. Indeed, there are eight primary defenses/excuses generally proffered and they range all the way from distorting the provisions of the law of war to various situational "excuses." All are equally fallacious.

The purpose of this book is to explore these so-called justifications and weigh them against the known facts and law. The conclusion is unequivocal – they are riddled with gross distortions, inaccuracies, and demonstrable falsehoods.

Considering that the war crimes on innocent noncombatant civilians were perpetrated not in some far-away land by foreign soldiers, but right here on American soil by American soldiers, the bankruptcy of truthful scholarship about the Union's premeditated use of terrorism in the Civil War should be of great concern to an enlightened public. While the most effective counterstroke to ignorance is to provide cold hard facts, it is certainly a sad sign of the times that even in an open and free society, people can be irrevocably propagandized and brainwashed.

While it is certainly right that all Americans should take great pride in the stellar conduct of their fighting men, be it the heroes at Valley Forge or Desert Storm, we must also be informed about the untoward stains on our national escutcheon. To do otherwise is not only intellectually dishonest but a certain guarantee that the same misdeeds will happen again in a future conflict. Only by acknowledging our failures can the appropriate "lessons learned" then be inculcated into our modern war fighters and leaders.[5] In other words, to properly navigate in the present or perform in the future one must truly understand the past. Accordingly, with the end of the longest conflict in American history – the twenty-year "War on Terror" – it is entirely efficacious to collectively look in the mirror of our history and explore the matter of Union terrorism to dispel the nightmarish illusion that it offered anything worthy of emulation or set a pattern of acceptable behavior for future conflicts. This largely untold story is worth the telling.

Finally, I am a proud 20-year veteran of the United States Army who not only spent most of my career as a senior legal advisor responsible for ensuring compliance with the law of war, but also had the good fortune to serve as the Staff Judge Advocate to the United States Army Special Forces Command (Airborne) – the Green Berets. Consisting of five active-duty Special Forces (SF) groups and two Army National Guard groups, the assigned duties of SF include direct action combat strikes against enemy forces and warfare training of allied indigenous forces – both missions heavily dependent on a strict adherence to the law of war and the highest levels of professionalism. As a subject matter expert in covering the requirements of the law of armed conflict, there is no greater satisfaction to witness how ethical conduct and combat efficiency go hand in hand.

Chapter One

DEFINING TERRORISM

The goal of the terrorist is to kill one and frighten ten thousand.[6]   *— Chinese Proverb*

THE CIVIL WAR was not just a series of large set piece battles fought between competing militaries with civilians watching from the sidelines. In the last two years of the war – particularly in the Western Theater – it degenerated into a shameful affair of command approved Union terror, striking out against tens of thousands of Southern noncombatants for the specific purpose of instilling fear and hopelessness across the larger general population of the Confederacy. Shamefully, the astonishing level of arson, theft, robbery, pillage, and even physical assault committed by Union forces in the 1864-1865 time frame was condoned at the highest levels of the Lincoln war machine.[7] It was command approved terrorism, pure and simple.

– What is Terrorism? –

Terrorism is nothing new. In the sphere of human history, the use of terrorism in warfare is a rather common phenomenon and is clearly on display for all the world to see in the 2022 Russian invasion of Ukraine. Reports of the Russian military targeting civilians in order to instill fear and hopelessness are rampant. Although many trace the etymology of the word terror to France's "reign of terror" under Robespierre and the Jacobin Committee of Public Safety (*regime de la terreur*), the employment of the tactic of terror is as ancient as human history.

Of course, before one can discuss a thing accurately, it must be defined. Unfortunately, when it comes to the matter of terrorism, this task is made difficult because, as in Lincoln's day, there exists no international consensus on a precise legal definition. Most likely this is due to the workings of the old cliché: "One man's terrorist is another man's freedom fighter." Accordingly, since all agree that the label *terrorist* unequivocally equates to criminal behavior, those who choose to employ the tactic during military operations, such as the Lincoln Administration, never describe their actions against innocent civilians as acts of terrorism, preferring instead to self-righteously cloak themselves with the "freedom fighter" mantle. Still, just as fact-based science doesn't care what *you* believe or wish things to be, acts of terrorism are acts of terrorism regardless of how they are painted or sugar coated. Terrorism is a crime or, more precisely, a criminal tactic whether employed in wartime or in peacetime.[8]

In the modern era, former Secretary General of the United Nations, Kofi Annan, proposed a wonderfully succinct definition of terrorism in the aftermath of the vicious 9/11 terror attacks on the United States by radical Islamic extremists. Although it was never adopted by the United Nations General Assembly, due to its rejection by the 56 member Muslim nation block, Annan's 2005 definition captured perfectly the common-sense elements of what terrorism is all about – it is most certainly an illegal action targeting civilians with physical violence for the purpose of making them do or refrain from doing certain acts. Annan's proposed United Nations definition:

[A]ny action constitutes terrorism if it is intended to cause death or serious bodily harm to civilians or non-combatants, with the purpose of intimidating a population or compelling a Government or an international organization to do or abstain from doing any act.[9]

Since the victims of terrorism in wartime are invariably innocent noncombatants, it appears fundamental that any common-sense definitional approach must concentrate on the illegal act itself, with the political, religious, or social reasons that motivated the act treated as matters of no valid interest whatsoever. This is precisely what Annan's definition did, omitting completely the idea that the "righteousness" or value of a particular cause could somehow excuse or even justify acts of terrorism. There is no "end justifies the means" trap door exception that would condone the use of terror. Terrorism is outlawed. Period.

Predictably, a ludicrous counter proposal to Annan came from certain member states advocating for a legal exception to justify terror tactics should the actions occur in the context of fighting a war of "national liberation." In short, it would be permissible to target innocent civilians with terror if the overall cause was just, in this instance to fight a former colonial power that maintained vestiges of influence in a third-world country. Since colonialism is "evil" any and all methods of violence would be permitted, even targeting civilians with violence and depredations. Similar to most apologists for the Union's use of terror during the Civil War – the cause was just – such twisted, nonsensical thinking killed the United Nations effort altogether.

Nevertheless, a customary international law approach most assuredly exists to draw upon. Under this regimen, the use of unlawful physical violence on civilians with intent to cause fear in a given civilian population to then influence a directed outcome is easily classified as a terrorist act. In other words, those who ransack and burn down private homes, violently assault innocent noncombatants, destroy private foodstuffs, slaughter domestic animals, take hostages, steal personal property, and so on are clearly engaging in acts of terrorism regardless of the underlying cause said to justify the attack, or whether the attack occurs in peacetime or during war. Whatever the cause for the criminal acts, terrorism can be described as making "war on civilians," a term correctly linked to Union General William T. Sherman, even though few seldom care to explain, let alone contemplate, the shockingly evil ramifications of what that repulsive phrase actually entailed.

In summary, to the common understanding of the general public, then and now, terrorism is the premeditated use of indiscriminate violence directed at innocent civilians in order to create a climate of fear which is specifically intended to influence or cause a desired outcome. This was certainly understood in Lincoln's day even though it was specifically prohibited in both the letter and the spirit of the Union's own law of war rules specifically drafted and adopted by the Lincoln Administration. Thus, the working definition that most civilized nations have adopted for their own domestic criminal code is patterned around three key characteristics:

1. The desire to cause fear in a given group of people to make them act in a particular manner.

2. The use of illegal acts of violence directed at civilians in order to achieve the goal at (1).

3. The continuing threat of future acts of illegal violence directed at civilians to further achieve the goal at (1).

As one would expect, terrorism against civilians is a tactic that is fully embraced by all totalitarian/authoritarian regimes but strongly rejected by democratic nations. The former has no regard for fundamental principles of decency and wields brute force to achieve their goals under a "law of the jungle" mentality, while the later embraces humanitarian concerns for all people and strives to operate under the rule of law in the conduct of warfare. For instance, in the War on Terror the enemy forces of radical Islam gleefully boasted of their gross acts of terror against innocent civilians, while the United States steadfastly conducted itself in combat operations under the strict dictates of the law of war, ever careful to employ lawful violence only against enemy combatants and not civilians. Even in the aftermath 9/11, when almost 3,000 innocent civilians were incinerated on American soil by Islamic jihadists, the United States did not seek revenge upon innocent Muslim civilians when it launched armed attacks against the al-Qa'eda and Taliban in Afghanistan later that year. Neither did the United States intentionally target civilians in its subsequent 20 years of military operations which saw other bloody battles in Afghanistan, Iraq, Syria, Libya, Yemen, Somalia, or any of the other nations that witnessed combat activities on their soil. This is not to say that individual American soldiers in their individual capacity did not commit acts of terror on civilians, they did, but those handful of miscreants were prosecuted under the Uniformed Code of Military Justice (UCMJ) for their crimes.[10] That's what civilized nations do. What never occurred in the War on Terror were *command directed* acts of brutality and terror against innocent civilians. This cannot be said for certain senior Union commanders during the Civil War.

– Why Use Terrorism? –

Why would a civilized nation such as the United States of America employ the use of terrorism on civilian noncombatants as it did during the Civil War? In fact, the Union's own rules and regulations approved by the Lincoln Administration as General Order 100 absolutely outlawed the use of terror tactics on civilians as violations of the law of war – war crimes.

The most common justification for Union terrorism – spoken or unspoken – was that terrorizing Southern civilians provided some level of contribution to an ultimate victory over the Confederacy. An outlawed construct under the law of war, it is still undeniable that whether Union terror tactics contributed to victory over the Confederacy or not, the long term social and political consequences were unquestionably harmful to national reconciliation and civil rights. Deviations from the moral formula of honorable conduct in warfare is destructive not only to the victim but also to the individual perpetrator and to the society he represents. Further, it is difficult for the Union to claim the moral high ground when their battle cry of "preserve the Union,"[11] and later, "free the slaves," is set against a backdrop of starving and destitute women and children silhouetted against burnt out homes and farms. In common military parlance: "The good guys, must act like the good guys."

If fear is the key ingredient in the equation of terrorism, cruelty is its calling card. But on a practical level, even apart from the immorality of brutalizing civilians, the tactic seldom finds validation, particularly when the targeted population possesses a stalwart inner courage and an unwavering commitment to the virtue of their cause. In short, terrorism doesn't always work. This phenomenon was certainly true when it came to the Confederacy. It is not an inaccurate observation that the Union's conscious decision to stoop to terrorism as part of a "total war" mentality actually had the opposite effect. Union terror only served to prolong, not accelerate, the surrender of the Southern armies in the field. It caused phenomenal misery to be sure, but in many crucial instances the tactic only stiffened, not weakened, the resistance of the Confederate people.[12] In the words of one historian:

> The psychological impact [of Union terrorism on civilians] should also not be overestimated. As evidenced in the tales of defiant Southerners watching the Yankees [plundering farms and homes] pass by, the destruction wrought in Georgia [on Sherman's March to the Sea] probably did as much to *harden hearts* as break spirits [emphasis added].[13]

— Right and Wrong —

It is for good cause that intelligent leadership in wartime demands that a "right thing must be done in a right way." This truism has long been an accepted norm for civilized democracies as reflected in the term *jus in bello*, which deals with the lawful employment of violence in war under the interwoven principles of military necessity, proportionality, and unnecessary suffering.[14] In short, the belligerents in combat may not lawfully use force against their opponents until these three factors are properly addressed. The first factor stands alone – a particular target must possess a direct military benefit to the enemy. Once this first element is established then the second and third factors are coterminous – the amount of force used to destroy said target must be proportionate and every effort must be taken to minimize unnecessary suffering, with particular focus on reducing collateral damage to noncombatant civilians.

Just as war is never fought unless the cause is just, *jus ad bellum*, this formula of lawful conduct in how combat is waged once it starts, *jus in bello*, is an essential ingredient for the perpetuation of a just society based on basic morality and the rule of law.[15] Accordingly, if one assumes that the stated cause of the Union to go to war was right – preserving the existing Union of States as one national entity – the intentional use of terrorism to achieve that goal was clearly wrong. A right thing done in a *wrong way* is wrong. The *jus ad bellum* does not provide a free license to ignore *jus in bello*.

Again, while the modern day peddlers of political correctness and anti-history make it difficult to use the Civil War as a teaching tool in discussing the subject of terrorism, it is beneficial that all Americans have a lucid understanding of the truth regarding the enormity of Union war crimes carried out by the premeditated use of terror in waging warfare against the Confederacy.[16] When General Sherman, the chief purveyor of terror and psychological warfare, equipped that "war is hell [for civilians],"[17] few today seem to comprehend the obvious ramifications of his statement – it was Sherman by his barbarous acts of terror, not the unintended consequences of collateral suffering that invariably occurs in warfare, that made it so *hellish*. The primary purpose of the law of war is to minimize the horrors of warfare as it affects innocent civilians, not to shrug off the horrors as expected outcomes or, as in Sherman's case, to actually celebrate it as a necessary scorched-earth policy against civilians.[18] The crucible that took so many lives was made far more hellish by the Union's cowardly use of terrorism on the innocents, many who were already widows and orphans, when the Federal soldiers came to brutalize them.

Nevertheless, while all civilized members of the human race would agree that such outrageous behavior by Union soldiers and their commanders was immoral *ab initio*, it is necessary to explore the issue of legality in greater detail. In other words, if there was no legally binding definition of terrorism at the time of the Civil War were those Union attacks against civilians nevertheless illegal under the law of armed conflict as it then existed? If such was the case then the terror tactics used by the Union would constitute gross violations of the law of war – war crimes.

Chapter Two

THE LIEBER CODE

Men who take up arms against one another in public war do not cease on this account to be moral beings, responsible to one another, and to God.[19] – Lieber Code

THE QUESTION AS TO whether or not Federal abuses against Southern civilian noncombatants violated the law of war, i.e., were war crimes, is relatively easy to address due to the fact that the United States specifically adopted a set of legal norms popularly known as the Lieber Code, which were formally codified by Abraham Lincoln into Federal law in 1863, as War Department General Order 100.[20] Thus, the formula is established. One need only measure the actual conduct of various Union forces in their employment of combat violence in light of their own rule of law!

The practice of war – when two nations engage in an international armed conflict – is regulated by a body of law known alternatively as the law of armed conflict,[21] or the law of war. The central purpose of the law of war has always been to mitigate the inevitable hardships attendant to warfare by:

> Protecting combatants, noncombatants, and civilians, from unnecessary suffering; [p]roviding certain fundamental protections for persons who fall into the hands of the enemy; particularly prisoners of war, military wounded and sick, and civilians; and [f]acilitating the restoration of peace.[22]

Under the current law of war, which consists of established customary principles[23] and international treaties, to include the 1949 Geneva Conventions,[24] all militaries must comply with this minimum threshold of behavior when conducting combat operations. There are no exceptions. Breaches are divided into simple violations, for minor offenses, and grave breaches for higher level violations such as murder, torture, arson, robbery, theft, and rape. In addition, each nation is under strict obligation to investigate any allegations of breaches of the law of war and to criminally prosecute all those who commit a grave breach. No exceptions.

At the beginning of the Civil War, the law of war that was binding on the American armed forces on both sides was actually not very different in form or substance from the key provisions which would be codified for the entire world in the 1929 Geneva Conventions, 66 years later. In fact, America's law of war at the time of the Civil War was directly patterned upon existing Prussian and British law of war codes, coupled with the long-standing customary humanitarian canons meticulously taught to young American officer cadets at the U.S. Military Academy at West Point.[25]

As it became apparent after a year of heavy fighting that the Confederacy would not easily be conquered, the Federal War Department sought to gather the various rules and customary practices concerning *jus in bello* into a single, uniform binding code for all its armies and asked Francis Lieber, a sixty-two-year-old German international law scholar and professor at Columbia College in New York, to lead the effort, with the Commanding General of the Union Army, General Henry Halleck, and three other generals also serving on the committee. Interestingly, Lieber was not only a well-respected academician, but he had honorably served as a solider in the Royal Prussian Army and fought against Napoleon at the battle of Waterloo. He was well-suited to lead the effort. The mandate:

> [T]o propose amendments or changes in the Rules and Articles of War and a code of regulations for the government of Armies in the field as authorized by the laws and usages of War.[26]

Given that there already existed a long-standing body of law in this arena of study to draw from, Lieber soon produced a rather comprehensive rule book that was shortly thereafter adopted by the War Department as: *"Instructions for the Government of the Armies of the United States in the Field."* Popularly known as the Lieber Code, the committee's work was officially promulgated and issued as a lawful order to all Union armed forces in May 1863, by means of General Order No. 100.[27]

The Lieber Code detailed out precise and fixed prohibitions juxtaposed with interpretive commentary and specific warnings concerning the lawful conduct of warfare. For instance, General Order 100 solemnly set the stage for all subsequent rules by proclaiming at Article 15:

> Men who take up arms against one another in public
> war do not cease on this account to be moral beings,
> responsible to one another, and to God.[28]

Although the Confederacy had already formulated their own military code of conduct for land warfare two years earlier, in 1861, entitled *"Articles of War, Regulations of the Army of the Confederate States,"*[29] Confederate Secretary of War James A. Seddon had no problem pledging to abide by the substantive provisions of the Union's Lieber Code. Like the bulk of the Union's law of war code, the Confederate Articles of War were also based directly on the well-established British system and accepted customs of war, so that the criminal subject matter jurisdiction of the Confederate military court-martial, "extended to offenses against the [Confederate] Articles of War [and] the customs of war."[30]

The Lieber Code consisted of ten sections broken down into 157 Articles.

Section I. Martial Law, Military jurisdiction, Military Necessity, Retaliation.

Section II.   Public and Private Property of the Enemy; Protection of Persons, and Especially of Women, of Religion, the Arts and Sciences; Punishment of Crimes Against the Inhabitants of Hostile Countries.

Section III.   Deserters, Prisoners of War, Hostages, Booty on the Battlefield.

Section IV.   Partisans, Armed Enemies not Belonging to the Hostile Army, Scouts, Armed Prowlers, War-rebels.

Section V.   Safe-conduct, Spies, War-traitors, Captured Messengers, Abuse of the Flag of Truce.

Section VI.   Exchange of Prisoners, Flags of Truce, Flags of Protection.

Section VII.   The Parole.

Section VIII.   Armistice, Capitulation.

Section IX.   Assassination.

Section X.   Insurrection, Civil War, Rebellion.

A central pillar of General Order 100 covered the humane treatment of civilians and their private property in time of war. While the requirement to treat civilians properly rests firmly upon an ancient foundation of humanitarian concerns which are intrinsically acceptable to civilized nations, the fact that such prohibitions are morally valuable axioms only captures part of the truth as to their development and utility. Clearly, the customary development of rules restricting violence against civilians and their property also follows a general pattern of what might be termed pragmatic necessity. Thus, the many rules prohibiting harm to civilians in General Order 100 finds logic in principles of self-interest, with the concept of reciprocity standing at the forefront. Thus, a belligerent military refrains from violations of the law of war upon the opponent's civilian population with the knowledge that the opposing military will do the same. In short, the soldiers in Lincoln's army were urged in exactly the same manner as the war fighters in today's American army to abide by "the principles and spirit of the law of war" on all military operations.[31]

Interestingly, the author of the Union's General Order 100 correctly asserted that the conflict between the Union and Confederacy was not a "civil war" under the legal definition. Professor Lieber commonly defined the term civil war as:

> War between two or more portions of a country or state, each contending for the mastery of the whole, and each claiming to be the legitimate government.[32]

As in America's War for Independence against England, the Confederacy never sought to overthrow the government of the United States to form a new country. The Confederacy was fighting for its independence from the United States and employed combat violence primarily in the context of self-defense from the aggressive intrusion of Union military forces upon its soil. In this view, the War Between the States was a second War for Independence and not a "civil war." However, just as the British would not consent to seeing their 13 colonies depart in 1776, so too Lincoln's Union would not let the 7, then 11, Southern States go in peace to exist as a new country. Clearly, Lincoln's previous position on the matter of secession when he was a congressman from Illinois had changed dramatically.[33] In a speech that haunted him, he stated in 1847, that any people or "a majority of any portion of such people" had the inviolate right to "shake off the existing government, and form a new one."[34] Power lust, quite naturally, has a peculiar way of changing people and Abraham Lincoln was no exception,

In any event, regardless of the "cause" of the War – from any perspective – the Lieber Code was concerned *in toto* with how the war was lawfully waged, stressing throughout that absolute theme of humane treatment for noncombatants. As a young man in the

Prussian Army Lieber had seen first-hand how the "inoffensive citizen of the hostile country" was brutalized in the various European wars. For instance, Article 25 stated:

> In modern regular wars of the Europeans, and their descendants in other portions of the globe, protection of the inoffensive citizen of the hostile country is the rule; privation and disturbance of private relations are the exceptions.[35]

— The Meaning of Military Necessity —

At the heart of the issue of proving that the Union committed command approved terrorism, i.e., war crimes, is the Lieber Code's definition of military necessity, a concept that related to three separate but closely interrelated themes when it came to distinguishing lawful combat violence from unlawful combat violence. First, although the Lieber Code correctly identified the valid concept of "military necessity," starting at Article 14 and following, which allowed for the destruction or capture of enemy soldiers and all government public resources used to sustain enemy forces,[36] called "military resources," the Lieber Code placed strict constraints on the use of that force when it came to encountering enemy noncombatant civilians.

In other words, while Article 21 recognized that the citizen of a hostile country was by definition an "enemy" and might suffer the normal collateral hardships of war,[37] Article 22 made it crystal clear that all enemy civilians were to be protected in their person and property as much as practicable.

> Nevertheless, as civilization has advanced ... so has likewise steadily advanced, especially in war on land, the distinction between the private individual belonging to a hostile country and the hostile country itself, with its men and arms. The principle has been more and more acknowledged that *the unarmed citizen is to be spared in person, property, and honor as much as the exigencies of war will admit* [emphasis added].[38]

Second, the Lieber Code also addressed in its concept of military necessity *vis a vis* civilian noncombatants those situations where it was essential for the belligerent military to impress needed supplies from them, but only in those instances where it was factually necessary under Article 15: "for the subsistence and safety of the Army."[39] In such exceptional cases of valid need for food and water for the belligerent soldiers, Article 38 provided additional restrictive requirements:

> Private property, unless forfeited by crimes or by offenses of the owner, can be seized *only by way of military necessity* ... [and] the commanding officer will cause receipts to be given, which may serve the spoliated owner to obtain indemnity [emphasis added]."[40]

In summary, when exercising the limited authority granted by military necessity to appropriate civilian property, General Order 100 absolutely prohibited any Federal soldier from engaging in larceny, vandalism, or indiscriminate burning of civilian private property as well as all associated crimes of physical violence against noncombatants. In very plain, strong, and unequivocal language, Article 47 of the Lieber Code mandated the following punishments for violators to include the death penalty:

> Crimes punishable by all penal codes, such as arson, murder, maiming, assaults, highway robbery, theft, burglary, fraud, forgery, and rape, if committed by an American soldier in a hostile country *against its inhabitants*, are not only punishable as at home, but in all cases in which death is not inflicted, *the severer punishment shall be preferred* [emphasis added].[41]

In turn, to completely underscore the importance of prohibiting illegal combat violence on civilians, Article 37 reinforced the requirement for protecting enemy noncombatant civilians when Union forces entered or occupied hostile territory:

The United States acknowledge and protect, in hostile countries occupied by them, religion and morality; strictly private property; the persons of the inhabitants, especially those of women: and the sacredness of domestic relations. Offenses to the contrary shall be rigorously punished ....[42]

In fact, Article 44 authorized superiors to shoot offenders "on the spot" for wanton violence on civilians.

All wanton violence committed against persons in the invaded country, all destruction of property not commanded by the authorized officer, all robbery, all pillage or sacking, even after taking a place by main force, all rape, wounding, maiming, or killing of such inhabitants, are prohibited under the penalty of death, or such other severe punishment as may seem adequate for the gravity of the offense. A soldier, officer, or private, in the act of committing such violence, and disobeying a superior ordering him to abstain from it, *may be lawfully killed on the spot by such superior* [emphasis added].[43]

Not only were enemy civilians to be protected from illegal combat violence, but the Lieber Code was also concerned with protecting certain "public" property necessary for the well-being of the civilian population such as hospitals, churches, universities, libraries, and museums. Even though the law of war certainly allowed for the destruction and appropriation of enemy government public property to include money, stores, fortifications, garrisons, moveable property, factories, and military resources, this was not a *carte blanc* to obliterate all "public property." Thus, churches, hospitals, schools, museums, and other property of a charitable character were excluded from the definition of enemy public property. Article 34 stated:

As a general rule, the property belonging to churches, to hospitals, or other establishments of an exclusively charitable character, to establishments of education, or foundations for the promotion of knowledge, whether public schools, universities, ... museums of fine arts, or of a scientific character – such property is not to be considered public property ... but it may be taxed or used when the public service may require it.[44]

Finally, there is the matter of the use of reprisals as a concern of military necessity, which the Lieber Code called "retaliation" at Articles 27-28. Reprisal or retaliation means that when one party to the conflict violates an established rule of law, the injured party has the right to respond proportionately with a use of force that otherwise would be unlawful. Thus, reprisals are not designed to punish the offending party, but to persuade the enemy to cease and desist the illegal conduct. In this vein, the offended party commits an otherwise illegal act but only for the sole purpose of getting the enemy to cease its prior commissions of gross illegalities in warfare. Furthermore, retaliation was only available when certain criteria were met.[45] At the time of the Civil War, the injured party would first have to provide a verbal or written warning to the wrongdoing belligerent. If the wrongdoer refused to comply with the warning to cease and desist the illegal conduct, then the injured belligerent could employ a response proportionate to the initial illegal act. Used only as a last resort, Lieber correctly warned that retaliation was a tool that if not used sparingly could rapidly lead to "the internecine wars of savages."[46] Article 27:

The law of war can no more wholly dispense with retaliation [reprisal] than can the law of nations, of which it is a branch. Yet civilized nations acknowledge retaliation as the sternest feature of war. *A reckless enemy often leaves to his opponent no other means of securing himself against the repetition of barbarous outrage* [emphasis added].[47]

Chapter Three

ADOPTING A POLICY OF TERROR

Do what you [General Grant] think needs to be done to win.[48] — *Abraham Lincoln*

WHEN PRESIDENT LINCOLN issued a call to each of the Union States to supply a quota of able-bodied men to form an army to put down the "rebellion," he included very strong language affirming the traditional and well recognized customary law of war proscriptions on the use of combat force when it came to civilians. On April 15, 1861, in his proclamation *Calling Forth the Militia and Convening an Extra Session of Congress*, Lincoln purposefully excluded any notion of "military necessity" which would allow for the taking or destruction of civilian property in the Southern Confederacy:

> [I]n every event the utmost care will be observed, consistently with the objects aforesaid, to avoid any devastation, any destruction of or interference with property, or any disturbance of peaceful citizens in any part of the country.[49]

However, with the subsequent adoption of the Lieber Code in April 1863, the important matter of "military necessity" was correctly addressed as a key component in the law of war, which did allow for the destruction and taking of civilian property if conducted in accordance with certain strong conditions attached. While Lincoln promulgated the Lieber Code into law, it is crystal clear from subsequent personal correspondence that he was more than open to operating outside of the strict humanitarian parameters of the Code, particularly when it came to dealing with noncombatants. For example, in an August 26, 1863, letter to a close friend, Lincoln openly approved of the destruction of property of innocent civilians even if done in violation of the Lieber Code. Apparently the only thing that Lincoln would find morally and legally objectionable in the Union's employment of combat violence was the murder of prisoners of war and innocent "noncombatants, male and female. Everything else was fair game. The letter is damning evidence that Lincoln would certainly look the other way when it came to enforcing the rule of law protecting innocent civilians.

> Is there—has there ever been—any question that by the law of war, property, both of enemies and friends, may be taken when needed? And is it not needed whenever taking it, helps us, or hurts the enemy? Armies, the world over, destroy enemies' property when they can not use it; and even destroy their own to keep it from the enemy. Civilized belligerents do all in their power to help themselves, or hurt the enemy, except a few things regarded as barbarous or cruel. *Among the exceptions are the massacre of vanquished foes, and non-combatants, male and female* [emphasis added].[50]

Although Lincoln's private views on war-making was legally and morally objectionable, the Union he presided over for the first two years of the armed conflict nevertheless conducted the War, more or less, in compliance with the law of war. Still, levels of Union atrocities against civilians accelerated without consequence and given Lincoln's expressed private view of what should be done to Southern civilians it was not surprising that no action to curtail the abuses occurred. In fact, on the very heels of the adoption of the Lieber Code, hundreds of reports of war crimes communicated directly to the highest levels of the Lincoln Administration simply fell on deaf ears. For example, in May 1863, Lieber himself wrote to General Halleck, the General-in-Chief of the Army (this position is equivalent to today's Chairman of the Joint Chiefs of Staff) in Washington:

I know by letters from the West and the South, written by men on our side, of course, that the wanton destruction of property by our men is alarming. It does incalculable injury. It demoralizes our troops, it annihilates wealth irrevocably and makes a return to a state of peaceful minds more and more difficult. Your order, though impressive and even sharp, might be written, with reference to the Code, and pointing out the disastrous consequences of reckless devastation....[51]

This particular warning to Halleck, who served as the top ranking officer in the Union Army from July 1862 to March 1864 (when Ulysses S. Grant took the job), is significant in many respects not the least of which is the fact that Halleck was required to report such matters to his boss the Secretary of War, Edwin Stanton (today's Secretary of Defense), as well as to President Lincoln himself.[52] In fact, there were streams of letters and communications bombarding the Lincoln Administration about the growing lawlessness in the Union armies over the treatment of civilians and their property. This is without serious debate. Indeed, William O. Stoddard, Lincoln's own secretary confirmed that all three men – Lincoln, Halleck, and Stanton – constantly kept in contact with each other on all matters pertaining to the War including the rising level of war crimes.[53] Stoddard noted:

Gen. Halleck is in constant communication and consultation with the President and Secretary of War ... the three work together in perfect harmony.[54]

Clearly, Lincoln knew what was happening. The growing abuses were so prevalent and widespread that it was literally impossible not to know. Instead of clamping down on the rampant abuses of the Lieber Code by his soldiers and commanders then operating across the South, the Commander in Chief was actually more in the mind of gearing himself up to abandon his moral compass entirely. With the exception of approving the outright murder of civilians, Lincoln would soon acquiesce to Sherman's repeated desires to conduct massive scorched-earth terror on innocent civilians in a manner never before seen.

– 1864 –

At the beginning of 1864, the situation for the Confederacy was bleak, but not entirely hopeless. To be sure, the opportunity for large scale offensive operations onto Northern soil were gone due to a lack of manpower and supplies, but if the embattled Confederacy could hold its own on Southern battlefields until the November elections, Lincoln and the Republicans might well be voted out and a peace treaty would follow. All the South had to do was to deny Lincoln a decisive victory which would surely sink his chances for a second four-year presidential term.

Due to a war weariness that had set in all across the Union, Lincoln himself shared this assessment causing the *New York Times* to write about a "manifest ebb in popular feeling throughout the entire country ... a regular period of despondency."[55] Not only had the Union military suffered 100,000 more casualties than the Confederacy, desertions were rampant spurred by a hatred of the unpopular draft and a laundry list of other concerns to include:

> [H]arsh suppression of dissent resulting in the suspension of the writ of habeas corpus in several states, imprisonment and even exile of opposition figures, and other constitutional infringements ... [along with Lincoln's] Emancipation Proclamation, [which] many outside New England rebelled against fighting other white men to free black slaves.[56]

Prone to spells of deep depression and extreme pessimism, President Lincoln actually wrote individual letters of apology to his own cabinet members and tucked them away in his desk drawer, anticipating his certain defeat at the polls in November 1864. Something more had to be done.

The deeply-religious South hoped and prayed that they might yet fend off the Yankee war of conquest. Deprivations were all too real and limited resources stretched to the breaking point, but the spirit of resistance burned bright in the people of the Confederacy. Things were going bad in the Western Theater, but, after all, they still had the indomitable Robert E. Lee in the Eastern Theater (most Northern newspapers were fixated on the War as it waged in the Eastern Theater).

General Lee inspired courage and hope in every soldier in the South and all Southerners remained absolutely confident that Lee would continue to pull off stunning victories as he had done so many times against Lincoln's large and well-equipped armies. While it was true that the much-vaunted Army of Northern Virginia had been forced back from Pennsylvania in July 1863, the Confederates still held onto much of Virginia and their capital at Richmond remained as defiant as ever. Every Union general that had come after Lee on Southern soil had been soundly whipped and sent scurrying back to Washington. For the Lincoln Administration, the repeated cry by the *New York Tribune* of "On to Richmond" was quickly replaced by the public with their own catch phrase, "It's a long road to Richmond."

In the Deep South, General Johnston protected the vital Confederate city of Atlanta with the battle-hardened veterans of the Army of Tennessee solidly dug in at Dalton, in northern Georgia. After Bragg's absolute debacle at Missionary Ridge in late 1863, the men were undeniably better commanded and, more importantly, ready and eager to fight.

The South was not about to quit. But the Union had a new general strategy as well as a new tactic to accompany it. Attack the Southern armies in unison and brutalize its people with wide spread terror.

— Grant's Grand Strategy —

In reward for taking Vicksburg and the striking victory at Missionary Ridge, Grant was catapulted to the top of the Union military's command structure, culminating with a promotion to Lieutenant General and the position of General-in-Chief of all United States forces (effective March 1864, the position formally held by Halleck). In short, Lincoln looked to hard drinking, cigar chomping, Grant to topple the Confederacy.

Always impatient in temperament, Grant had actually cut down on the alcohol, but not the cigars, and in late 1863, he formulated a simple and methodical grand strategy to subjugate the South. Unimaginative in design, the plan was not a swift knock-out blow as had been attempted in the past by so many other overconfident Union generals, but a long game of strangulation that took full use of the North's far superior muscle. The strategy centered on amassing and then employing the tremendous advantage the Union held in manpower and resources to simply grind down the armed forces of the Confederacy in a bloody war of attrition. No one quick victorious thrust to the heart, just a series of deep gashes all across the corporate body until the South literally bled to death. Regardless of the number of casualties, civilian or military, required to accomplish the goal of total subjugation Grant intended to launch more or less simultaneous attacks by all the major Union armies in the field – then 21 army corps consisting of approximately 533,000 men – against the major Confederate armies. Again, nothing fancy or brilliant in the plan or the execution, each Federal force would just bunch up in a tight porcupine-like mass and move slowly forward against their far weaker opponents. Furthermore, with these huge movements synchronized, each of the Southern armies would be individually overwhelmed as Richmond would not be able to shift forces from one army to another as was done with the Confederate victories at Manassas in 1861 and Chickamauga in 1863. One historian described Grant, who many considered a long way from smart, and his method of warfare as follows:

> Grant was not a particularly imaginative strategist. Grant believed in increasing the weight of the army he brought to bear upon the enemy's defenses until they snapped like an overburdened shelf. He plotted the eruption of men he would need to overflow the landscape.[57]

The main drawback to Grant's all engaging plan of placing the Rebels in such desperate straits was obvious. Because the Federals would be on the offense Union casualties would be horrendous. This did not faze Grant in the least because he knew that the United States could easily replace the losses – immigrants were pouring off the boats in New York by the tens of thousands – while the South could not, a fact that was particularly vital when it came to Lee's Army of Northern Virginia. In fact, Grant's Union Army of the Potomac almost drowned in its own blood during the summer of 1864, losing more men fighting Lee than Lee had in his entire army! Although Grant would never admit it, even to himself, he pragmatically understood that Lee was by far the superior general on the field of combat. But Grant also understood that he could afford to strike hard and lose battles longer than Lee could keep winning them. Impervious to Northern cries that Grant was a butcher of his own men, he coldly calculated that, sooner or later, Lee would run out of men and material. Lee was the fox, but Grant would plod ahead and push like the elephant as he had done in the Vicksburg campaign in 1863.

In any event, the entire premise for the coming slaughter of 1864, would require far more blue-clad men than was currently on hand. Lincoln would soon be obliged to call up another half million draftees – right on the heels of the hated Federal Draft Act of March 1863, which had sparked massive riots in New York City and the largest number of lynching's of black Americans in history.[58]

Consisting of three legs, the grand movement would kick off in the spring of 1864, when the weather sufficiently warmed. It would play out as follows. In the far west, Union General Banks would move out with his combined army from New Orleans with the limited objective of capturing the "blockade running" port city of Mobile. Sherman would strike out against Johnston who was covering Atlanta. Grant would go after the main prize of R. E. Lee, who was covering Richmond from the Rapidan River.

The two main Federal armies in the east that Grant would personally oversee were the Army of the Potomac, commanded by General Meade, and the Army of the James, commanded by General Ben "Beast" Butler. As a collateral effort against Lee, Grant also ordered Union General Sigel to advance another smaller Federal army into the Valley to prevent any reinforcements or foodstuffs from going to Lee's embattled troops. In addition, Sigel was specifically authorized to employ open terror tactics on Southern farmers which included burning down any and all civilian crops in the farm rich Shenandoah Valley and destroying all civilian farms and homes at will.

In the lower South, General William T. Sherman would bundle three separate Union armies across Tennessee, into a massive "army group" of 100,000 plus. This army would drive straight into northwest Georgia to crush General Joseph E. Johnston's much smaller Army of Tennessee consisting then of only two depleted corps totaling about 40,000 – one under Lieutenant General William J. Hardee and the other under Lieutenant General John Bell Hood.[59]

– Lincoln's Two Policies of Suffering –

While readily approving Grant's military strategy to simultaneously attack the two main Confederate armies, Lincoln chose to look the other way when Grant implemented two other collateral policies – each one a horrid construct of heartlessness that shocked the conscience. "More important, a new type of warfare was being planned – total war."[60]

First, in order to further weaken the ability of the Confederacy to replenish their numbers in the field, Grant drastically reduced the volume of prisoner of war (POW) exchanges with his Confederates counterparts. Grant knew that with 85% of the white male population in the South already in uniform, prisoner exchanges were the only source the Confederacy had to replenish their depleted ranks, unless they enlisted black Southerners to bear arms. In contrast, the North had no such manpower problems and simply drew from an endless supply of young fresh-faced draftees, many foreign born. In addition, the Lincoln Administration had finally agreed to enlist tens of thousands of black Americans into active military service, a move that greatly assisted the Union war effort.

Without debate or objection from Lincoln the Union policy of halting POW exchanges was implemented with a cold and deadly calculation and little regard to its deadly impact on their own soldiers. Everyone knew that such a move would spell horrible suffering and death to thousands upon thousands of Union prisoners. The South could not feed its own troops in the field let alone the multitude of new Union prisoners that would soon flood into their hands with the upcoming Federal offensives of 1864. The Union's halt to prisoner exchanges directly contributed to the tragic misery at Andersonville and other Confederate POW camps during 1864-1865. It was simply beyond the means of the South to properly feed and care for them.

Lincoln's willingness to sacrifice his own soldiers penned up in horrid POW camps meshed perfectly with the second newly approved policy to prosecute the War. The Lincoln Administration now allowed the use of wide scale terrorism on innocent Southern noncombatants in the belief that the impact would cause the families, soldiers, and government to once and for all stop resisting the Union invasion and surrender.

Although Grant and others in the hierarchy of command were always careful to disguise the new terror policy with colloquialisms, everyone fully understood that civilians and their property were now fair game. Sherman knew exactly what Grant was suggesting, for example, when Grant slyly substituted the normal term "war materials," used for the lawful combat activity of destroying such things as military warehouses, supply depots, railroads, and forts with a new term (not found in any civilized law of war codes and in point of fact specifically outlawed by the Lieber Code) which he coined for using illegal combat violence against civilians and their private dwellings – "war resources."

Sherman was well pleased with Grant's plan, but wanted assurances that Lincoln approved of the part that Sherman would soon play in targeting civilians with wholesale destruction. He messaged Grant on April 2, 1864: "I would like to have the President's Consent before I make my orders." A week later, Grant replied in the affirmative and on April 10, greatly satisfied that he had the green light from Lincoln to conduct his "Enlightened War," i.e., operate outside the Lieber Code against civilians, Sherman wrote a private letter to Grant in which he stated:

> Your letters of April 4 are now before me, and afford me infinite satisfaction. That we are now *all* [Lincoln, Grant, and Sherman] to act a Common plan ... looks like an *Enlightened War* [emphasis added].[61]

With Union terror now officially sanctioned, Lincoln had abrogated his responsibility to ensure discipline and lawfulness in his military. He simply sat on his hands, and remained generally silent with no hint that he sanctioned the atrocities. However, following Sherman's massive scorched-earth movement across Georgia to the port city of Savannah, Lincoln did tip his hand that he approved. President Lincoln sent a personal letter of congratulations on December 26, 1864, slyly stating that he had acquiesced to all that had happened.

> Many, many, thanks for your Christmas-gift—the capture of Savannah .... Now, the undertaking being a success, the honor is all yours; for I believe *none of us went* farther *than to acquiesce* [emphasis added].[62]

Chapter Four

WAR CRIMES NORTH

[W]e are not only fighting hostile armies, but a hostile people, and must make old and young, rich and poor, feel the hard hand of war, as well as their organized armies.[63]　　　　　　　　　—*William T. Sherman*

WHEN LINCOLN ANNOUNCED his invasion of the Confederacy, the general public in both the South and the North anticipated a short war, perhaps a single battle or two and then it all would be over. Others, like Stonewall Jackson and Lee, had no such illusions; they saw a protracted and bloody fight against numerically superior invading armies.

Largely owing to its vast industrial might, when the War began the Federals held tremendous physical advantages at their disposal. Although the standing United States Army in 1860 consisted of only a mere 16,000 professional troops spread out all across the nation, the North could claim over "22 million people compared to the Confederacy's 9 million, only 5.5 million of whom were white."[64] Interestingly, the loyal Union States had about 430,000 slaves while the Confederacy had about 260,000 free blacks in their general population. More importantly, greater than eighty percent of the military-age white male population in 1860 lived in the areas that remained with the Union – to include the four Union slave States of Missouri, Kentucky, Delaware, and Maryland. In addition, the North enjoyed the benefits of an unlimited supply of new immigrants (almost 800,000 enlisted in the United States military during the War) which were readily available as replacements to feed into the

Union meat grinder.[65] In fact, about a quarter of all Union troops were foreign born, with the largest immigrant group being German, followed by the Irish.

Lincoln's initial theory for conquest was direct. He would raise a large army by requisition from the loyal States and then invade and crush the Confederacy by capturing the Rebel capital in Richmond and ending the matter of Southern independence that very year of 1861. The fallback strategy, if needed, was called the "Anaconda Plan" proposed by then General-in-Chief of the U.S. Army, the venerable Winfield Scott. Scott's two-part strategy envisioned a long conflict and called for blockading all the salt water Southern ports to cut off foreign supplies and then move to seize control of the Mississippi River. As the name implied, this would cut off and then strangle the Confederacy's ability to acquire or produce the essential components and materials needed to defend itself.

– Total War –

Violations of the law of war occurred on both sides during the conflict, but relative to the Union's command approved abuses which launched in earnest in 1864, as part of Grant's strategy to end the War, the Confederacy's record of wrongdoing pales in comparison. While the South may have to endure the stigma of the renegade William Quantrill who terrorized the Missouri and Kansas countryside with his small gang of bandits (Union ruffians also did the same in Missouri),[66] in the minds of many Americans – particularly in the South – the name of William T. Sherman is immediately associated with a most heinous array of war crimes that were carried out on a massive scale and shocked the conscience of the civilized world. From his February 1864, Meridian campaign in Mississippi, to his infamous March to the Sea later that year, and then to the horrific burning spree through South Carolina, Sherman maliciously employed a strategy that intentionally and blatantly used terror to inflict unnecessary suffering on tens of thousands of noncombatant civilians, primarily the elderly, women, and children. Sherman called his scorched-earth policy "total war."[67]

The actual method of Sherman's making *total war* on ordinary people involved the command directed use of his formidable army not only to burn down countless private dwellings and steal all types of personal property, but to actually strip the local countryside of all the food and livestock necessary to sustain life and cultivate new crops. The worst of it came from lawless gangs of roaming blue-clad marauders, called "Blue Devils," or bummers, who shamelessly engaged in indiscriminate plunder and acts of outrage upon a defenseless civilian population – black and white, rich and poor.[68] In fact, most of the despoiled victims were the families of poor non-slave owning yeomen farmers.

In turn, along with these widespread criminal acts came the inevitable excesses committed by the morally bankrupt elements imbedded in the Union army. Seeing the extreme latitude given by Sherman towards terrorizing the populace, these types were quick and eager to extend the terror factor even further and committed individual atrocities which included sexual assault, robbery, torture, and even murder. According to a friendly biographer of Sherman who sought to distinguish Sherman's foragers from the others, these "men pillaged, burned and raped their way to the coast completely out of control."[69]

Accordingly, whether loosely approved by Sherman under his infamous order to his soldiers at the start of the march across Georgia to "forage liberally," or simply allowed by turning a blind eye and looking the other way, the wanton acts of Union terrorism arguably marks Sherman as one of the most infamous figures in American military history. As one noted historian observed:

> The history of warfare furnishes few examples of forbearance by the invading troops, while *the extent and character of the depredations committed have usually reflected the attitude of the commanding general* and the discipline, or lack of it, in the enlisted ranks [emphasis added].[70]

While other Union leaders employed similar acts of terrorism, the miscreant Sherman was the *uber* proponent of employing the tactic during the Civil War. A graduate of West Point and well-schooled in the legal requirements of civilized warfare, Sherman nevertheless came to believe that such atrocities against the common Southern civilian were somehow needed in order to vanquish the Confederacy. Without compulsion or remorse, Sherman blatantly ignored the letter as well as the spirit of the Lieber Code, despising such rules as inconvenient impediments to his vicious machinations.

– An Evolving Policy –

In the first year of the War the policy of ruthless terror toward Southern civilians was not condoned by the Lincoln Administration, although many in the Northern press voiced strong rhetoric about ignoring abuses if such should occur. Instead, wishing to avoid a protracted conflict Lincoln concentrated his main effort on a quick capture of the Rebel capitol which had been moved from Montgomery, Alabama, to Richmond, Virginia, in April 1861.[71] But as the months passed into years and the Confederates under Robert E. Lee beat back every Union advance towards their capitol, concerns mounted.

To be sure, many Union commanders were well aware that by late 1863, the "unwritten" policy from Washington was increasingly weighted to "look the other way" when it came to reports about Union forces "living off the land," i.e., pillaging the foodstuffs and livestock of Southern country people. Acknowledging this green light from Washington, Sherman simply supersized things on a grand scale of abuse and with Grant elevated to supreme commander, the horrific tactic of making war on vast swaths of civilians took root as the *modus operandi* for the troops under his command. For instance, the disturbing atrocities described in Sherman's July 1863, letter to his wife Ellen about his soldiers pillaging Jackson, Mississippi, would soon pale compared to what was to come for the noncombatants of Georgia and South Carolina. Sherman gleefully described the conduct of his soldiers whom he had turned loose to sack the Mississippi capital:

[T]he soldiery proceeded to *sack the town completely*. Pianos and articles of furniture were dragged into the streets and demolished. The *aroused soldiers entered residences, appropriating whatever appeared to be of value* ... those articles which they could not carry they broke .... They thrust their bayonets into pictures and knocked out windows and even removed doors from their hinges [emphasis added].[72]

Far from being shocked by her husband's flagrant admission of Union savagery and his feigned inability as a general officer to control his own *aroused* soldiers, Mrs. William T. Sherman knew full well that Sherman himself directed the crimes, and she wholehearted approved and egged him on to perform even greater acts of savageness. In one of her many hate filled letters against the South she responded in kind to her husband, reminding him that the Union's motive for invasion was not to free slaves (both were extremely racist) but to put down the rebellion by targeting the Southern people with unrelenting vengeance. Ellen implored:

I hope this may not be a war of emancipation [of the slaves] but of extermination, & that all under the influence of the foul fiend may be driven like Swine into the Sea. *May we carry fire and sword into their states till not one habitation is left standing* [emphasis added].[73]

– Blood and Fire –

By early 1864, the Union military had made significant inroads in their goal to conquer the Confederacy, without resorting to large scale acts of scorched-earth terrorism against Southern civilians. With the fall of Vicksburg in July 1863, the Federals controlled the entire Mississippi River and R. E. Lee had been turned back at Gettysburg that same month. Despite these significant strategic victories, however, all was not well for the Lincoln Administration. From a political perspective, it seemed that the "peace platform" of the Democrat party would sweep the fall 1864 elections putting

Lincoln and the Republicans out of office and power. As related in Chapter Three, Lincoln knew that the United States was extremely war weary and Lee's Army of Northern Virginia remained firmly in place protecting Richmond, while the still dangerous Rebel Army of Tennessee protected Atlanta.

Realizing that his election to a second term in office in November 1864, was contingent on a significant deliverable blow signifying the imminent defeat of the Confederacy, Lincoln grew increasingly exasperated and finally agreed with Sherman and his ilk that the use of terrorism against noncombatant civilians was necessary to cripple the South's morale and will to continue to resist. With what amounts to a policy of "blood and fire,"[74] Abraham Lincoln was willing to sacrifice law, morality, and decency itself if it meant his victory.

Lincoln acquiesced to those subordinates who embraced Sherman's "rule of the jungle" warfare on civilians. Lincoln washed his hands and left it to Grant and his senior generals to "[d]o what you think needs to be done to win."[75] Casting aside his own General Order 100, which he had previously praised in 1863, Lincoln took to "unofficially" condoning actions specifically designed to terrorize civilians as part of the evolving Union strategy to demoralize, drain, and ultimately defeat the Confederacy. The Southern women and children posed no direct threat to Union forces – there was no "military necessity" to brutalize them – but that was irrelevant to the new ruthless war strategy. Thus, the Confederate soldier's mother, wife, daughter, and sister whom he had left behind to tend the home and farm were now directly targeted for horrid depredations seldom paralleled in the annuals of civilized warfare. In turn, many enslaved black Southerners who had "guarded anticipation" about Lincoln's promise of freedom suffered as well and had those thoughts "often replaced with a sense of betrayal as they suffered along with their owners, complicating their decision of whether to flee with or from the Union troops."[76]

If caught in the path of Sherman's advancing soldiers, not only were all their foodstuffs and personal valuables stolen or utterly destroyed, many were subjected to physical assault and although never commanded, an unknown number of innocents were sexually molested by criminal elements within the Yankee rank and file. It was blatant terrorism pure and simple and the newly promoted Lieutenant General William T. Sherman (as of late 1864), now in full command of the three main Federal armies in the Western Theater, would not only practice terrorism but revel in it during his march from Atlanta to Savannah and then through South Carolina.

Each day as Sherman's army moved forward marauding terrorists known as "bummers," apparently a disparaging word of German origin, were detached from individual regiments and sent on ahead with empty wagons to "forage liberally" off the local homes and farms of the women, children, and elderly of the South. Some were wealthy plantation homeowners, but the vast majority were just small farms occupied by those who were barely able to scratch out a living now that their men were all off fighting. A bummer raiding party could be as large as fifty or as few as ten and would often be attended by a junior officer. Because the men in the individual regiments took turns at this mission, which all viewed as a pleasurable break from the monotony of marching in dusty columns of four, "virtually every man in Sherman's army, at one time or another, participated in a foraging expedition."[77] Indeed, as the march progressed and all understood that there would be no adverse consequences for the pillaging – particularly given that the majority of the atrocities were conducted in the wide open countryside – it was not uncommon for entire companies and even regiments to detach themselves from the main column of march to indiscriminately plunder, so that looting bands of vandals often outnumbered the foragers. All was done with the utmost enthusiasm.

Even the main body of the Federal army engaged in depredations similar to what was practiced on the outskirts of the movement. Those towns, villages, and homes that had the misfortune of standing in the direct path of the main infantry force were invariably wiped off the face of the earth. One of Sherman's staff officers, Captain Pepper, chronicled the usual routine when the entire wing surged into or near a particular town or village. They were not "living off the land," they were razing it.

A halt at noon beside a village, a besieging of houses by the troops, soldiers emerging from doorways and backyards, bearing quilts, plates, poultry and pigs, beehives attacked, honey in the hands and besmearing the faces of the boys, hundreds of soldiers, poking hundreds of bayonets in the corners of yards and gardens, after concealed treasure; here and there a shining prize, and shouting and scrambling and a merry division of the spoils. *In the background women with praying hands and beseeching lips unheeded* [emphasis added].[78]

Another eyewitness to the immediate aftermath of the main Union army on the move recorded that for forty miles she did not see a single rail fence, let alone a standing structure, but only the rotting carcasses of countless domestic animals killed for spite.

The fields were trampled down and the road was lined with carcasses of horses, hogs, and cattle that the invaders, unable either to consume or to carry away with them, had *wantonly shot down to starve out the people* [emphasis added].

As twisted as Sherman may have been in his soul, it is beyond naïve to conclude that he carried out these war crimes without the full knowledge and approval of his superior and friend General Ulysses S. Grant. But then again, Lincoln could disingenuously feign ignorance far easier than Grant. Sherman's many tirades concerning abusing and destroying Southern civilians went directly to Grant. But Sherman was not alone, he was just the most prominent.

The 1864 Union policy of terror against civilians reverberated far and wide with other Union commanders to include Robert H. Milroy in Tennessee as well as Philip Sheridan and David Hunter in Virginia's Shenandoah Valley.[79] For instance, in 1864, General Robert H. Milroy was assigned the critical job of keeping the vital Union held railroad in Tennessee open and running. A spitefully evil human being, Milroy sought to halt Confederate hit and run cavalry attacks on the railroads by seeking revenge on every Southern home that happened to be in the proximity of a particular Rebel cavalry strike, which sometimes included out and out murder of any civilian male occupant in that home. In point of fact, hundreds of civilians in Union occupied Tennessee thought sympathetic to the cavalry raids were murdered by Federal troops, right on their own property. While most were simply gunned down in cold blood, a not uncommon practice was to hang the victim by the neck from his own door yard and to then pull on the dangling legs to ensure death. In describing how he dealt with what he called "Confederate sympathizers," Milroy wrote to his wife Mary, disgracefully mocking a Biblical salvation passage from the New Testament – Acts 16:30-31.[80]

> *Blood and fire* is the medicine I use. I *shoot the men* who are friendly with and harbor bushwhackers [Confederate cavalry] and *burn their houses.* By spreading death and fire in a neighborhood where the bushwhackers have a friend, the survivors come rushing in terror *"What must I do to be saved?"* [emphasis added].[81]

Another commander who engaged in the vile practice was Union Major General Philip Sheridan. With Lincoln's full knowledge, Sheridan's soldiers completely burned out all the civilian farms in Virginia's beautiful Shenandoah Valley during 13 days in August 1864, conducting a methodical scorched-earth operation known to this day as "The Burning." This was done under direct orders from General Grant:

> *Eat out Virginia clean and clear* as far as they go, so that crows flying over it for the balance of the season will have to carry their own provender with them [emphasis added].[82]

For his part, Sheridan happily complied, later stating his pleasure at inflicting so much suffering on the innocents. He continued similar atrocities against civilians for the remainder of the War, echoing Grant and Lincoln's view that the primary purpose was to break the people's will to support the Confederacy.

– The Terrible Mind of Sherman –

There is no question that the most notorious Union general in the context of the use of terror against Southern civilians was William Tecumseh Sherman, a sinister-looking fellow with dark chilling eyes, who may not have used actual bullets against civilians as in fighting regular enemy soldiers, but did not hesitate to invoke raw ferocity on defenseless women and children through arson, theft, and pillage. To intentionally employ the Union army to terrorize civilians was something that Sherman urged early on, even contending that the War must go on until "enough southern landowners [civilians] were killed off [murdered]."[83]

Although Sherman pushed out significant terror attacks on civilians during his Meridian, Mississippi, campaign in early 1864, it was only a precursor of larger horrors to come – it would be his March to the Sea across Georgia in the fall of 1864, that would forever place him at the high table in the annals of infamy. After Atlanta was captured in September 1864, Sherman hatched a scheme to move his veteran army across the heartland of Georgia, two hundred and eighty-five miles, to the seaport city of Savannah. With General Hood's Army of Tennessee transferred off into Tennessee, Sherman knew he would face no greater opposition than a few thousand cavalry and some old men and boys from the Georgia State militia. This meant that he was absolutely free to do as he pleased. Sherman proposed to methodically spread out his men in a wide marching swath of 60 miles, designed to terrorize as many civilians as possible, and rip his army across the countryside. The South had been penetrated before by invading Union armies, but never despoiled in the manner that Sherman sought.

On September 10, 1864, General Sherman telegraphed his boss U. S. Grant for tentative permission to conduct his nefarious plan to target the "houses and people" of Georgia. At first Grant was reluctant, but permission was soon granted and Sherman wired General Thomas in Nashville, Tennessee, on October 2, 1864, that he intended to gather between 60,000 and 65,000 men to devastate Georgia in order to "make its *inhabitants* feel that war & *individual*

Ruin are synonymous terms [emphasis added]."[84] Sherman also sent a chilling message to Grant on October 9, 1864, leaving no doubt about what was in his mind to do.

> Until we can repopulate Georgia, it is useless to occupy it; but the *utter destruction of its roads, houses and people* will cripple their *military resources....* I can make this march and make *Georgia howl* [emphasis added].[85]

Chapter Five

FALSE JUSTIFICATIONS

War is simply Power unrestrained by Constitution or Compact.[86]   – *William T. Sherman*

AS ANY SERIOUS STUDENT of historical events knows, depending on one's "interpretation" of history, there can be alternate and even conflicting versions of the past. This phenomenon is particularly evident in how many historians choose to view the Union's use of terror tactics in the Civil War.

While Sherman's widespread war crimes committed during his military movement in the Deep South are incontrovertible, most apologists for his wide spread employment of terror prefer to either remain silent or, in the alternative, to deny the cold hard facts of what actually occurred. On the other hand, as with the case of Sherman himself, some have foisted a variety of sophomoric "defenses" to cover up and/or justify the terrorism and war crimes. Indeed, there are eight primary defenses generally proffered and they range all the way from distorting the provisions of the Lieber Code to various situational "excuses." All are equally fallacious to justify the acts of terror perpetrated against Southern civilians by other Union forces during the War. When these so-called justifications are weighed against the known facts, they are riddled with gross distortions, inaccuracies, and demonstrable falsehoods. The eight excuses/ defenses for the marauding, arson, pillaging, and other depredations against noncombatant civilians are as follows:

1. First, the Lieber Code's allowance for destroying "military resources" of the enemy is disingenuously amended with a made-up phrase termed "war resources," which now includes all Southern civilians and their property as lawful targets for destruction.

2. Second, distorting the Lieber Code's limited allowance for confiscating civilian property under "military necessity," Sherman is painted as a commander in dire need of sufficient food stuffs and provisions required to sustain his starving army on its 300-mile march behind enemy lines.

3. Third, the devastation Sherman wrought against civilians was not that bad.

4. Fourth, although Sherman was the commanding general and issued specific written orders outlawing all forms of depredations, he could not control his soldiers, either because of their great lust for pillaging civilians or, alternatively, because he was ignorant of the magnitude of the war crimes that were occurring at the time.

5. Fifth, Sherman was bravely operating behind enemy lines boldly risking everything in the face of a vibrant Confederate military force that opposed him at every step allowing little opportunity to ensure the safety of civilians harmed along the way as a matter of collateral damage by his swift moving army.

6. Sixth, the so-called terror tactics that Sherman used were actually lawful at the time and setting of the American Civil War.

7. Seventh, Sherman was only following superior orders from Grant and bears no direct or indirect culpability for the crimes against civilians.

8. Eighth, the end justifies the means. The Lieber Code and any other law of war proscriptions outlawing terrorism are irrelevant because achieving a military victory over the Confederate States of America had to be achieved by any means necessary, to include terror tactics on innocent civilians.

– False Justification One: Destroying War Resources –

When Sherman sought formal approval for the operation to march from Atlanta to Savannah, General Grant certainly understood that he would have to euphemistically disguise the true purpose of the terror campaign. Grant knew full well that what Sherman proposed was far beyond the law of war under the Lieber Code's stringent definition of taking civilian property when required by *real* military necessity or destroying military resources which directly benefited the Confederate government. Pillaging and burning civilians out of their homes was an entirely different matter and some fancy double-talk by Grant was sorely needed.

In fact, Grant had already overcome this problem earlier by duplicitously coining the term "war resources," when he had ordered Sherman on April 2, 1864, to attack General Johnston's Army of Tennessee then stationed at Dalton, Georgia. Along with aggressively hitting the Army of Tennessee, Sherman was instructed to simultaneously inflict maximum damage to enemy "war resources" – Grant's new term to justify targeting civilians and their property. Grant had simply conflated the lawful targeting of the enemy's public property under the Lieber Code, termed *military resources*, such as trains, government storehouses, military bases, and manufacturing plants with the newly invented term *war resources*. Thus, war resources now included noncombatant civilians and their property. They were magically made legitimate game for combat styled violence. In other words, irrespective of the rule of law, Southern civilians and their property were redefined as key components of the Confederacy's military resources and subject to immediate destruction by any means necessary. In this manner, the Union military was not illegally pillaging and burning homes and farms, they were simply destroying war resources of the Confederacy. Grant instructed Sherman:

> You propose to move against Johnston's army, to break it up and to get into the interior of the enemy's country as far as you can, inflicting all the damage you can against their *war resources*. I do not propose to lay down for you a plan of campaign, but simply to *lay down the work it is desirable to have done*, and leave you free to execute in your own way [emphasis added].[87]

Although Sherman was limited in his scope of committing depredations against civilians prior to the fall of Atlanta in September 1864, primarily due to constant combat with sizable Confederate military forces, that was all going to change. Grant reemphasized the term "war resources" in his one sentence approval for Sherman to strike out into the interior of Georgia. This time, however, Grant knew that Sherman would face no significant military opposition which might hinder fulfilling the malicious goal of terrorizing civilians, although he would sometimes fret when reading the propaganda from Southern newspapers about how Sherman would meet his doom. In fact, General Grant didn't even mention to Sherman the possibility of confronting Confederate armed forces as he knew it was irrelevant. He simply ordered Sherman to "get into the interior of the enemy's country"[88] and destroy as much of the civilian homes and farms as he could.

While granite faced Sherman was not a savvy as Grant when it came to covering his tracks to conceal true intentions, it is debatable whether Grant himself would have condoned in advance the *degree* of atrocities and terror that Sherman actually perpetrated against civilians on his march across Georgia. In any event, there can be little doubt that Grant and Lincoln had a pretty good idea of what was in Sherman's mind, they had known it all along as evidenced by the fact that neither ever criticized his terror tactics before, during, or after it was over. In conclusion, this justification is pure double-talk.

Fact: It is fundamentally clear that the twisted *war resources* phrase was in complete and utter violation of the Lieber Code's prohibition of targeting noncombatant civilians with unlawful combat violence.

— False Justification Two: Military Necessity —

For his part Sherman was vicious, heartless, and not as politic as Grant, but he was not entirely dull of thought. Understanding that he could not officially go on record ordering terror attacks on civilians, regardless if it was disguised as an effort to eradicate so-called war resources as Grant put it, he skillfully played Orwellian word games of his own to justify his war crimes. To employ a modern jingle of the delusional "woke culture," Sherman took to *reimagining* the Lieber Code's definition of military necessity. After all, the Lieber Code allowed for the taking of enemy civilian property in those cases where it was required to sustain an army in need of foodstuffs and supplies while operating in the field. Despite the fact that Sherman was awash in all sorts of sundries and supplies that had come down by the tonnage via the Union controlled rail from Tennessee, he unilaterally declared that he was in desperate "need" of food for his army on the march and had to take it from the people of Georgia as his troops moved across the State – *military necessity*. In his memoirs, written a decade after the War, Sherman actually asserted this exact fallacious claim.

> [N]o army could have carried along sufficient food and forage for a march of three hundred miles; so that foraging in some shape was necessary.[89]

This view is also parroted by many writers on the topic to include Lee Kennett in his book, *Marching Through Georgia*.

General W. T. Sherman, 1865.

It was Sherman who conceived of the march and who argued successfully for it. Since the operation *could only be carried out by drawing sustenance from the population*, from the moment his project was agreed to, the desolation of some portion of Georgia was assured [emphasis added].[90]

Accordingly, a week before leaving Atlanta, on November 9, 1864, Sherman penned Special Order Number 120 which authorized his army to *"forage liberally* on the country [emphasis added]."[91] Claiming that his new order was legal under the doctrine of military necessity – to obtain needed supplies from the civilian population while on his movement across Georgia – it was nothing more than an ill-fitting cover slogan to shield him from criticism. As detailed in Chapter One, the legitimate use of the doctrine of military necessity *vis a vis* civilians dealt primarily with two separate scenarios. The first allowed for the destruction of privately owned civilian property in certain rare instances where there existed a direct military value to the enemy, i.e., akin to destroying *true* military resources used by the belligerent government. Such lawful targets might include privately owned railways, privately owned salt mines, privately owned lumber mills; or privately owned clothing factories. It certainly did not include privately owned dwellings and property.

The second allowed for the taking of private civilian property if needed to actually sustain a starving army while in the field. Again, this would only be in special circumstances where the army ran out of food due to emergencies caused by such things as extreme weather or unexpected enemy actions against supply depots. However, both uses of the doctrine of military necessity were viewed as rare exceptions to the overarching general rule enshrined in the Lieber Code which repeatedly emphasized protecting the private property and persons of all enemy noncombatants.

For instance, the first scenario under military necessity is found at Article 44 of the Lieber Code. Article 44 specifically allowed for the destruction of private property upon the order of an officer if that property was considered of *direct* value to the enemy. To underscore this point, the granted exception was worded in the negative – "all destruction of property not commanded by the authorized officer ... are prohibited" – which meant that it was not to be construed broadly against civilians in general even if justified in certain individual instances.[92] Even so, if Article 44 allowed the means for an officer to authorize an otherwise illegal act, Articles 14 through 16, by setting out strict definitions of the term military necessity, certainly limited an officer's ability to even issue such commands in the first place. Most certainly, to destroy a civilian home or farm and take all foodstuffs and animals would never be considered as an action that constituted "*direct* value to the enemy." Article 14 states:

> Military necessity ... consists in the necessity of those measures which are *indispensable* for securing the ends of the war, and which are *lawful according to the modern law* and usages of war [emphasis added].[93]

As previously covered, Article 15 of the Lieber Code did allow for the "appropriation of whatever an enemy's country affords *necessary for the subsistence and safety of the Army*" [emphasis added],[94] under an emergency scenario, but specifically required that the owners of such property be given money or receipts for their lost goods so that they could seek reimbursement at a later date. This too was never done.

In any case, in practice and by his own written admissions penned on numerous occasions, Sherman consciously and intentionally with malice aforethought violated the quintessential requirements regarding the lawful and limited use of military necessity as set out in Article 16 of the Lieber Code. His actions personified "cruelty."

> Military necessity *does not admit cruelty* – that is, the infliction of suffering for the sake of suffering or for revenge, nor of maiming or wounding except in fight ... *nor wanton devastation of a district*. It ... does not include any act of hostility which makes the return to peace unnecessarily difficult [emphasis added].[95]

How can Sherman defenders not define burning private homes, shooting all the farm animals, and stealing all the foodstuffs as a prima facia case of pure unadulterated *cruelty*? Furthermore, Sherman's scorched-earth methods against whole swaths of civilian territory absolutely constitutes "wanton devastation of a district."

The strongest evidence which negates Sherman's twisted application of military necessity to appropriate private foodstuffs from civilians, let alone loot and pillage their homes and destroy their animals and crops, comes from the Union's historical record itself. Always a meticulous logistician, the facts reveal that Sherman actually carried with him out of Atlanta all the food and supplies that his almost 65,000-man army would ever need to traverse across the State of Georgia. In point of fact, when Sherman departed Atlanta in November 1864, having burned the remaining homes and businesses to the ground, he methodically calculated that it would take about 30 days of marching to reach Savannah and carried along with his army more than enough provisions to make the trip. Indeed, with good weather on his side, Sherman reached the half-way mark in his journey only ten days out from Atlanta.[96]

In the months since his army had occupied Atlanta, he was able to draw on the unlimited source of supplies via the Union controlled rail line from Tennessee to amass a phenomenal stash of food and supplies. So that when his army left Atlanta, Sherman took along with him 2,500 newly built U.S. military supply wagons, pulled by 25,000 horses and mules, which "carried 1.2 million rations of hardtack and enough pork, coffee, salt, and sugar to last forty days."[97] Well-guarded, this wagon trail extended almost 25 miles! Sherman also took along a herd of 10,000 beef cattle and enough forage for the animals to last at least five days – plenty of time to clear the ravaged countryside immediately in the vicinity of Atlanta. Of course, with the looting and pillaging, these supplies were barely used. For example, Union Major Hitchcock recorded in his journal that with all the men "in the rebel army" absent from their homes in Georgia Sherman's men were free to loot and burn at will. He noted that the theft and robbery was so rampant and widespread that even after having traveled about 100 miles in the march none of the 10,000 cattle they had brought had been butchered. Hitchcock wrote:

> Large numbers of cattle, mules, etc., picked up, "acquired" the phrase is, today: some fine ones. J.C.D. says he has not yet killed one beef out of the droves we brought along. At every farm house is plenty of corn, stacks of fodder, vats, etc.: plenty *till this army* had passed.[98]

The record shows that after only two days of looting Sherman's army had more stolen food than it could possibly use for the next thirty days! Faced with such historical truth, there is no question that his mission to pillage the people of Georgia was one of pure unadulterated vengeance and cruelty in direct contravention of Article 16. General Sherman openly and intentionally targeted unarmed women, children, and the elderly to make them suffer for having supported and continuing to support the Confederacy, rather

Sherman's soldiers pillaging civilian homes.

than any necessity to feed his troops.[99] Indeed, as previously covered, if there had existed a valid need to confiscate civilian property, there were very strict protocols in place concerning the requisitioning of food which not only included issuing receipts but, more importantly, leaving enough for the subsistence of the property owner(s) who were to be unmolested and allowed to remain secure in their own homes. Sherman ignored it all.

Whether terrorized by the roaming gangs of bummers and looters who rampaged at will or the ravenous main Union army that destroyed everything in its path, no pay or script of any kind was tendered the owners for what was "appropriated." Even more dastardly and shocking, what was not stolen was burned or killed and left to rot so that the starving civilians were left with little or nothing to eat.

For the troops it was unrestrained looting. After stuffing themselves with every form of plunder from a given home and barn, the surplus provisions collected would be whisked back to the main column to be feasted on by the particular regiment that had sent them out. All knew that Sherman's mandate to forage liberally was not only permission to take private foodstuffs to allegedly feed the army but doubled as a license to despoil, steal, and burn as they wished. Their mission was to destroy and terrorize.

In summary, given the fact that Sherman carried with his army sufficient Union wagons stuffed full with provisions aplenty to completely sustain his entire force on the 30-day march to Savannah, there was absolutely no need to exercise the taking of civilian property under the legitimate reading of military necessity, let alone engage in a vicious "live off the land" campaign that had nothing to do with either military necessity or humanity. It was pure terrorism. In fact, so much plunder was brought back to the main body to eat that the majority of that food was simply abandoned to rot on the roadside.

At the core of the argument for this false justification is Sherman's claim that since no "army could have carried along sufficient food and forage for a march of three hundred miles,"[100] military necessity allowed for him to "live off the land." This is a falsehood and easy to refute. The fact that he did carry along "sufficient food and forage for a march of three hundred miles" constitutes the most damning evidence against the preposterous claim of military necessity.

Fact: While securing forage for the limited number of Union animals might have qualified under the Lieber Code for limited requisitions from a few civilian farms along the way, Sherman actually did carry along with him more than enough food and supplies for his soldiers to easily make the short 300-mile movement.

— False Justification Three: It Wasn't that Bad —

A third justification focuses on the amount of destruction wrought by Sherman. Proponents state that relative to other miscreant armies and commanders in both earlier and later wars in human history, Sherman's actions weren't *that* bad. In addition, they say, one must simply ignore the general's vicious rhetoric and other rantings about destroying and exterminating people. For example, in the preface

Union soldiers pillaging civilian homes.

to a multi-volume set on the Civil War, the author defends General Sherman and his soldiers with simplistic reasoning that borders on the ludicrous:

> [He] did not authorize a scorched-earth policy, even though families had to struggle to find food in the wake of his armies ... there was pillaging, to be sure, yet Sherman's soldiers did not murder civilians, nor did they destroy *all the towns* in their path [emphasis added].[101]

First, of course Sherman did not overtly authorize "a scorched-earth policy" in writing. No American commander would ever officially authorize such horrors. He simply and whole heartedly encouraged and allowed it by his overt inaction. Then the author admits that "families had to struggle to find food," but fails to mention why that had happened. For the author the good news is that "Sherman's soldiers did not murder civilians" and didn't destroy *all* the towns, just most of them!

While it is certainly true that the scale and scope of what Sherman did cannot be compared to the likes of Genghis Khan or Adolph Hitler, he nevertheless seated himself at the same table of infamy by intentionally waging uncivilized and illegal violence against civilians to a level heretofore unseen in American history. The suffering was widespread and vicious. In fact, Sherman ignored American law and looked instead to the European model of the Middle Ages with great approval, where civilians were generally spared their lives, but little else. Speaking of his Atlanta campaign, Sherman told a friend that his terror actions would "compare well with that of the European Models."[102]

Despite the reluctance of defenders of Sherman to actually examine the historical record concerning the degree of abuse, one thing is certain, the victims of Sherman would find little consolement to discover that the Yankees had spared one or two of their neighbors' houses along the way. A Wisconsin private perfectly described the true results of Sherman's terror policy to his wife:

> On the march [through Georgia] ... there is not enough left in the country to support the women and children. This is a wicked, damnable, accursed war; if you could see and hear the poor women and innocent children crying and begging that we leave them a little meal or something to eat; yet the last morsel would be taken and they left to suffer.[103]

Looking at the hundreds of letters and journals from both the sponsors of terror and the victims of terror reveals that the typical scenario in both Georgia in 1864, and then in South Carolina in early 1865, played out as follows. Upon arriving at a particular farm, the soldiers would feed themselves first, forcing the women – black or white – of the household to cook them a full meal as they rudely lounged about the private dwelling. Next, having filled their stomachs, the thieves masquerading as law-abiding soldiers would coarsely rampage through every drawer and corner of the family home looking for valuables such as silver, gold, or jewelry. Then they would fan out across the property and collect the dried meat along with the stored foods in the sheds or cellars to fill their forage wagons, killing and butchering on the spot the family cows or any other farm animal they seized. All horses and mules were targeted for immediate theft and whatever animals were not stolen

Union soldiers pillaging civilian homes.

were killed right where they stood for spite, always over the cries for mercy from the women left with nothing to feed themselves or their young children. Adeline Jackson, an enslaved person in South Carolina, recalled these vandals:

> The Yankees that I remembers was not gentlefolks. They stole everything they could take and the meanest thing I ever see was shoats [pigs] they half [*sic*] killed, cut off the hams, and left the other parts quivering on the ground.[104]

Often the Union soldiers would use threats and outright violence to make black and white civilians reveal hiding places that might contain valuables. In many instances, the black Southerner was treated far worse in this regard. For instance, it was common practice for Sherman's soldiers to place a revolver to the head of any loyal servant and "threaten to shoot him unless he disclosed the whereabouts of the goods."[105] Former enslaved American Andy Marion of Winnsboro, South Carolina, recalled his own unlucky encounter with Sherman's troops:

What did the Yankees do when they come? They tied me up by my two thumbs, try to make me tell where I hid the money and gold watch and silver [dinnerware], but I swore I didn't know. Did I hide it? Yes, so good it was two years before I found it again. I put everything in a keg, went into the woods, spaded the dirt by a pine stump, put the keg in, covered it up with leaves and left it.[106]

Finally, after the wrecking, killing, and stealing was completed the torch was applied and every structure was burned to the ground to include the dwelling house and any barns or sheds on the property. While burning private homes occurred with great frequency in Georgia, every home the Federals reached in South Carolina was burned to ashes. If possible, depending on the dry weather, any remaining corn crops still in the field were also set ablaze. To further terrorize the destitute women and children, the departing Yankees would even "cut all the well ropes and st[eal] the buckets."[107] Ben Leitner, another former enslaved American recalled his experiences.

When the Yankees come, they ransack the house for silver and gold. They burn the house and gin-house; carry off mules, horses, and cows. They took the chickens, load all the provisions, put them in a four-horse wagon, and *leave us and the white folks cold and hungry. It was cold wintertime then too* [emphasis added].[108]

These scenes of terror were repeated over and over as cold and shivering young mothers stood by in helpless shock. Sherman was well pleased with the results and in many cases only the chimneys, called Sherman's sentinels, remained as mute testaments to the crimes against humanity. A typical letter penned by a woman visited by Sherman's blue-clad vandals illustrates the sheer terror experienced by all.

Sherman has gone, and terrible has been the storm that has swept over us with his coming and going.... There was no place, no chamber, trunk, drawer, desk, garret, closet, or cellar that was private to their unholy

eyes. *Their rude hands spared nothing but our lives
... squad* after squad unceasingly came and went and
trampled through the halls and rooms of our house
day and night during the entire stay of the army. At our
house, they *killed every chicken, goose, turkey, cow,
calf, and every living thing, even our pet dog.* They
carried off our wagons, carriages, and horses, and broke
up our buggy, wheelbarrow, garden implements, axes,
hatchets, hammers, saws, etc., and burned the fences.
Our smoke-houses and pantry – that a few days ago
were well stored with bacon, lard, flour, dried fruit, meal,
pickles, preserves, etc. – now contain nothing whatever,
expect a few pounds of meal and flour, and five pounds
of bacon.... One of these barbarians had to add insult to
injury by asking me *"what you would live upon now*?" I
replied, "Upon patriotism [emphasis added]."[109]

The truth is that the vast majority of the dwellings and towns
were not spared. In the vast majority of encounters with his soldiers,
all the property and personal belongings of the elderly, women, and
children were destroyed. Conducted in the dead of winter, this *is* the
very definition of "scorched-earth."

While defenders of Sherman refuse to comprehend the depth of
the terrorism, as members of Sherman's infantry or cavalry visited
their homes, defenseless Southern civilians quickly understood
what Sherman's version of warfare entailed. In the distance, as
the Yankees approached, they could see the pillars of smoke by
day and the fires by night. As frightened women and children
deciphered the movement of the blue juggernaut, the dirt roads
were soon jammed with fleeing families carrying everything they
could in small, dilapidated wagons. All empty homes were quickly
burned with Sherman's approval, as he considered them abandoned
property. Those that could not escape were swallowed up and left
completely destitute, wandering and begging across Georgia in the
cold wintertime.

The quantity of illegal destruction was horrendous. According to one well respected historian, the out and out theft of civilian food and property was staggering.

> Altogether, Sherman's foragers took from the country a staggering amount of food, fodder, and animals. From Georgia alone they confiscated [stole] 6,871 mules and horses [slaughtering on the spot many times over that number], 13,294 head of cattle [slaughtering on the spot many times over that number], 10.4 million pounds of grain [burning on the spot many millions more pounds], and 10.7 million pounds of fodder as Georgia farmers unwillingly contributed almost 6 million rations of beef, bread, coffee, and sugar to the Union infantry and artillery [and cavalry].[110]

Sherman himself happily estimated that he destroyed 100,000,000 worth of property in Georgia and "admitted that eighty percent of this was simple 'waste and destruction.'"[111] Even a half-century later, the effects of Sherman's war crimes were still felt in the areas he devastated. Exploring in detail all the relevant economic and census data in the decades that followed Sherman's terror march in Georgia reveals that it took until 1920 for those areas to fully recover.

> As late as 1920, agricultural investment in Southern counties in the 10-mile-wide path of devastation lagged behind investment in counties that were spared.[112]

Fact: The terrorism wrought by Union command approved policies were horrendous in nature and widespread in scope, devastating the lives of tens of thousands of innocent civilians in a way heretofore unseen on American soil.

– False Justification Four: I Can't Control My Army –

After burning the entire city of Atlanta to the ground, Sherman set out on November 15, 1864, with about 65,000 hardened Federal soldiers, not to engage Confederate combat forces, but in his own words to "make Georgia howl."[113] Taking a malignant satisfaction in his plan of devastation, Sherman methodically spread out his army into two wings so that it could cover thirty miles on each end for a total destructive kill zone of sixty miles across as it burned and terrorized through the land to the Atlantic Ocean. Miles and miles of charred landscape would mark the passage of the Union soldiers who were freely allowed to rob, pillage, and burn.

Although Sherman did issue Special Order Number 120 which self-righteously prohibited the trespass of all private dwellings, required the leaving of reasonable provisions for families who were forced to provide food to his men, and even prohibited the use of profane language, in reality none of these things were enforced.[114] In terms of protecting civilians, Sherman's General Order 120 was a total farce:

I. For the purpose of military operations this army is divided into two wings, viz, the Right Wing, Maj. Gen. O. O. Howard commanding, composed of the Fifteenth and Seventeenth Corps; the Left Wing, Maj. Gen. H. W. Slocum commanding, the Fourteenth and Twentieth Corps.

II. The habitual order of march will be, wherever practicable, by four roads, as near parallel as possible and convergent at points thereafter to be indicated in orders. The cavalry, Brigadier-General Kilpatrick commanding, will receive special orders form the commander-in-chief.

III. There will be no general train of supplies, but each corps will have its ammunition train and provision train distributed habitually as follows: Behind each regiment should follow one wagon and one ambulance; behind each brigade should follow a due proportion of ammunition wagons, provision wagons, and ambulances. In case of danger each army corps commander should change this order of march by having his advance and rear brigades unencumbered by wheels. The separate columns will start habitually at 7 a.m., and make about fifteen miles per day, unless otherwise fixed in orders.

IV. The army will *forage liberally on the country* during the march. To this end, each brigade commander will organize a good and sufficient foraging party, under the command of one or more discreet officers, who will gather, near the route traveled, corn or forage of any kind, meat of any kind, vegetables, cornmeal, or whatever is needed by the command, aiming at all times to keep in the wagons at least ten days' provisions for the command and three days' forage. *Soldiers must not enter the dwellings of the inhabitants, or commit any trespass*, but during a halt or a camp they may be permitted to gather turnips, potatoes, and other vegetables, and to drive in stock in sight of their camp. To regular foraging parties must be instructed the gathering of provisions and forage at any distance from the road traveled [emphasis added].

V. To army corps commanders alone is entrusted the power to destroy mills, houses, cotton-gins, &c., and for them this general principle is laid down: In districts and neighborhoods where the army is unmolested no destruction of such property should be permitted; but should guerrillas or bushwhackers molest our march, or should the inhabitants burn bridges, obstruct roads, or otherwise manifest local hostility, then army commanders should order and enforce a devastation more or less relentless according to the measure of such hostility.

VI. As for horse, mules, wagons, &c., belonging to the inhabitants, the cavalry and artillery may appropriate freely and without limit, discriminating, however, between the rich, who are usually hostile, and the poor or industrious, usually neutral or friendly. Foraging parties may also take mules or horse to replace the jaded animals of their trains, or to serve as pack-mules for the regiments or brigades.

In all foraging, of whatever kind, the parties engaged will refrain from abusive or threatening language, and may, where the officer in command thinks proper, give written certificates of the facts, but no receipts, and they will endeavor to leave each family a reasonable portion for their maintenance.

VII.   Negroes who are able-bodied and can be of service to the several columns may be taken along, but each army commander will bear in mind that the question of supplies is a very important one and that his first duty is to see to them who bear arms.

VIII.   The organization at once of a good pioneer battalion for each army corps, composed if possible of Negros, should be attended to. This battalion should follow the advance guard, should repair roads, and double them if possible, so that the columns will not be delayed after reaching bad places. Also, army commanders should study the habit of giving the artillery and wagons the road, and marching their troops on one side, and also instruct their troops to assist wagons at steep hills or bad crossing of streams.

IX. Capt. O. M. Poe, chief engineer, will assign to each wing of the army a pontoon train, fully equipped and organized, and the commanders thereof will see to its being properly protected at all times.

By order of Maj. Gen. W. T. Sherman:

L.M. DAYTON

Aide-de-Camp

Apart from the obvious conclusion that Sherman was a detailed micro-manager who was completely involved in every aspect of his vast army, the humanitarian words sprinkled throughout the order were mere window dressing designed to camouflage the acts of terror

A Union "bummers" returning to their units after pillaging civilian homes.

to come. In truth, the only part of General Order 120 that stuck with his men was the illegal command to: "forage liberally on the country" – Sherman's euphemism for pillaging and plundering. General Order 120's soothing platitudes were only lovely smokescreens for the gullible of his time and for those in future generations smug in their willingness to accommodate the lies. All along Sherman was intent on engaging in a scorched-earth movement and his soldiers immediately caught on to the true meaning of the order, as illustrated by the following episode which occurred early on, just outside Atlanta, when a disheveled and intoxicated Union infantryman loaded down with plunder sarcastically looked Sherman in the eyes and gleefully echoed the general's own command back to him. A nearby subordinate recorded the incident, for which Sherman took no corrective action.

> [The soldier had] a ham on his musket, a jug of sorghum-molasses under his arm, and a big piece of honey in his hand, from which he was eating. He said [noticing Sherman], "forage liberally on the country."[115]

Another Union officer dryly observed the obvious consequences of Sherman's open license to forage liberally which created a "morbid appetite to take things ... [making it] impossible to restrain some from carrying the thing to the extreme."[116] Impossible, of course, because Sherman absolutely refused to enforce his own orders!

Despite Sherman's phony pro forma directives vowing protection to civilians – to include outlawing bad language – the reality was far different and Sherman purposefully intended it to be exactly that way. Again, Sherman perfectly understood that by turning a blind eye to the outrages he had given his tacit approval for terror. His General Order 120 simply protected his hide and he was often keen to remind his post-war critics that he had expressly prohibited, in the strongest language, no "cursing," pillaging or depredations. Of course, prohibiting on paper is far different than enforcing the prohibitions.

In fact, throughout the entire march to Savannah not a single evening role call was made in any of the separate companies as they halted for the night, a required and standard good order and discipline military protocol which allowed for the officers to account for, inspect, and control their men, and in this new environment of traversing through civilian territory, to reinforce the humanitarian requirements of the Lieber Code,[117] or for that matter his own General Order 120. None of this was done. Why? Because Sherman did not desire good order and discipline when it came to terrorizing innocents.

Inflamed by his own criminal power lust, Sherman unleashed his soldiers so that inhumanity and hatred ruled the day with every foul deed imaginable committed against defenseless civilians time and time again. Those with a propensity towards criminal behavior were certainly the most vicious, allowed to do just what they pleased with little or no consequences, but then again everyone took a hand in the depredations at one time or another.

In many ways, the men who carried out Sherman's terror tactics were not different from the very civilians they terrorized. The majority of Sherman's soldiers were from the Midwest and many grew up in rural environments, working with their hands, tilling the fields, raising farm animals, and going to Protestant church services on Sunday. They did not need the legalistic mandates set out in military law and the Lieber Code to tell them right from wrong, but they were certainly savvy enough to understand Sherman's true intent to deal violently and harshly with Southern civilians. In addition, they were soldiers. Given a green light from their superiors, the rank and file obeyed. Coupled with a numbness born from repetition of the crimes, few were able to resist a growing group think about the validity of engaging in wanton destruction. No doubt, it was an exhilarating experience for the men to loot and burn without fear of punishment and most were willing participants in a carnival of evil. One Union solider recorded: "We serve all [civilians] alike, use partiality to none of them for we take everything."[118] Clearly, however, although not all the Union soldiers engaged in atrocities on the innocents, the results were universal. A Union chaplain in Sherman's army put it best when he wrote:

> I do not mean all the [Union] men rob houses, but all the houses are robbed.[119]

To be sure, military discipline not enforced quickly leads to degeneracy in conduct among the many. Sadly, the fearless behavior of the Federal soldiers on the battlefield fighting the valiant men of the Confederacy was forever tarnished by their cowardly behavior in debasing the helpless women and children of the South.

Like the Wisconsin infantryman in Sherman's command who blamed the commission of wholesale crimes on the "accursed war,"[120] and not on his fellow soldiers or commanders who committed them, General Sherman would sometimes express a sense of helplessness to stop the terrorism, as if the actions of his own soldiers was somehow beyond his ability to influence.[121] Major Henry Hitchcock also regretted the fear, anxiety, and terror visited on the women, but he certainly understood that the blame was with Sherman alone rather than the so-called "accursed war." Hitchcock knew that Sherman could stop the outrages at any time. He wrote in his journal:

I am sure that a Headquarters Provost Marshall, with a rigid system of roll-calls in every company required at every halt – severe punishment inflicted not only on men who straggle but also on officers who fail to prevent it ... would go far to prevent these outrages.[122]

Hitchcock added in his diary that Sherman was fully aware of the terrorism carried out by his soldiers and that he intended it to be exactly so. Confiding to Hitchcock on the third night of the march out of Atlanta about a defenseless woman who had earlier begged him for protection from his soldiers. Sherman denied her request knowing she would be horribly abused by his men.

I'll have to harden my heart to these things. That poor woman today – how could I help her? There's no help for it. The soldiers will take all she has.[123]

Sherman understood everything that *his* soldiers were doing, although some proponents of the "it was not so bad" class will foist a bait and switch argument by attempting to differentiate between Sherman's "foragers" and the work of the "bummers." Some writers even go further and include in the category of bummers not only Sherman's Federal troops, but Georgians, Confederate deserters, and even regular Confederate cavalry forces who were opposing Sherman's march – anything to take the spotlight off of Sherman and his now reimagined "good" soldiers. For example, in the popular multi-volume work *The Civil War* put out by Time/Life books one finds the following:

Worse than the regular foragers were unsanctioned gangs of renegades and looters ... and they were probably responsible for a majority of the rapes committed during the march.[124]

Of course, such ridiculous conjecture is pure magical thinking. That Sherman sponsored the depredations and that the vast majority of the crimes were committed by his soldiers is without serious debate as evidenced in his remarks to Major Hitchcock in offering the false choice between acknowledging the Confederacy's right to exist as a nation or directing the "plundering, burning, and killing" by his men to force it back into the Union.

> Either we must acknowledge the "C.S.A." or we must conquer, we must make war, and it must *be* war, it must bring destruction and desolation, it must make the innocent suffer as well as the guilty, it must involve plundering, burning, killing, Else it is worse than a sham.[125]

On another occasion, when Hitchcock confronted Sherman about the burning of the city of Marietta, Georgia, to the ground, Sherman nervously smacked his lips and quipped that "[President] Jefferson Davis was responsible,"[126] not him. Sherman flippantly elaborated:

> Set as many guards as you please, they will slip in and set fire .... I never ordered burning of any dwelling – didn't order this, but can't be helped. I say *Jeff Davis burnt them.*[127]

At other times, Sherman openly expressed great delight with the results of his terror policy and would boast about how he had "turned loose" the soldiers so that they could commit wholesale looting and burning. In fact, eagerly anticipating the repetition of his Georgia terror policy that he intended to next carry into South Carolina, Sherman even wired General Grant about how all *loyal* Americans would approve of his criminal tactics of turning loose his soldiers to terrorize the civilian population wholesale.

> I sincerely believe that the whole United States, North and South, would rejoice to have this army *turned loose* on South Carolina, to *devastate that state in the manner we have done in Georgia* [emphasis added].[128]

Like Lincoln, Grant was silent about Sherman's blatant admission of authorizing war crimes and terror. In fact, concerning South Carolina, Sherman instructed one of his generals, Henry Slocum, that he was not to spare any private property from the flames because the civilian noncombatants had to be "punished."

> You need not be so careful there [South Carolina] about private property as we have been. The more of it you destroy the better it will be. The people of South Carolina should be made to feel the war, for they brought it on and are responsible more than anyone else for our presence here. *Now is the time to punish them* [emphasis added].[129]

Indeed, after completing his month-long movement through Georgia and snuggly headquartered in the finest mansion in Savannah, Sherman corresponded regularly with his superiors in Washington concerning his upcoming march through South Carolina. Since his army was waiting in place at Savannah during the last months of winter, Sherman did not destroy the city. However, as if attempting to shed all responsibility for his past atrocities in Georgia and mitigating his responsibility for the future war crimes that he fully intended to commit when he later moved into South Carolina, Sherman telegraphed Major General Henry Halleck, now the Chief of Staff, another confession of future terror.

> [T]*he whole army is burning with an insatiable desire to wreak vengeance upon South Carolina.* I almost tremble for her fate, but *I feel she deserves all that seems in store for her* [emphasis added].[130]

Of course, Abraham Lincoln was fully aware of the telegraphs that reached Washington about the conduct of the War. By then he knew all about the horror Sherman had brought to the civilians in Georgia. Lincoln said nothing and did nothing as he read Sherman's phony declaration about his helplessness to discipline or control his forces from massive criminal behavior.

Strangely, it must not have occurred to Sherman that no commander worth his salt would ever affirm such obvious weaknesses in leadership skills – admitting a complete loss of disciplinary control over his own command – unless, of course, he actually desired that precise outcome. Just as the historical record refutes his use of "military necessity" to pillage civilians, it also affirms that Billy Sherman had complete and total control of his army at all times and in all circumstances.

In reality, Sherman exercised an iron-fisted control over his men – when he wanted to. When Sherman ordered the army to pack up and move out on a march, the troops would immediately stop pillaging and do exactly as directed, even if many grumbled that it impeded their licentiousness. Examples of this fact are numerous but perhaps the best illustration of Sherman's firm and total grip over the conduct of his soldiers occurred during his earlier Meridian terror campaign in February 1864.

Having allowed his troops to literally burn and pillage their way from the Union garrison in Vicksburg all the way to Meridian, Mississippi, Sherman turned his 35,000-man army around and headed back towards Vicksburg, but this time by a route that targeted fresh areas not burned and hollowed out by his outgoing movement. While making the return trip, Sherman decided to halt his army for a few days at Canton, Mississippi, near the Pearl River, about 70 miles from Vicksburg. However, on the night of February 25, before crossing the Pearl River and entering the town with his entire army, Sherman "abruptly changed his policy in regard to burning, looting, and leaving families destitute."[131] General Sherman issued detailed and definitive commands to both his division commanders, Major General McPherson and Major General Hurlbut, and sternly ordered them to enforce his new directives with an iron hand, no exceptions. Both subordinate generals snapped to and sent immediate orders to their respective divisions prior to entering Canton the next day. McPherson's General Field Orders No. 6 read in part:

Division, brigade, regimental, battalion, and detachment commanders are required to have this order so thoroughly disseminated that every officer and solider will be unable at any time to plead ignorance in excuse for violation of the same.

The order will be read in the hearing of every officer and solider at least three times, and the fact reported to these headquarters at 6 p.m. on the 26th instant.

First, no house, cotton-gin, or building of any description will be burned or destroyed unless by special orders from these headquarters.

Second, *no officer or soldier will be permitted to enter any house or other building* unless by special orders from these headquarters, division, or brigade headquarters.

Third, *no foraging party will be sent except by special orders from division or brigade headquarters*, and then the names of the officers in charge will be registered at the headquarters of the brigade or division to which they belong, in order that any misconduct or violations of this order on the part of officers or men may be properly reported and the offender summarily dealt with [emphasis added].[132]

Sherman forced this most out of character order to his men because he had abruptly decided not to personally wait in Canton along with his troops for a hoped-for link up with a missing body of 8,000 Federal cavalry (unknown to Sherman, Nathan Bedford Forrest had already defeated and driven the hapless Federals back into Tennessee), but to press on by himself with a small cavalry escort to Union held Vicksburg. His army would stay in place for a while, but Sherman was restless to return to Vicksburg to plot out his next campaign.

Coterminous with the new order enforcing civilized behavior in strict compliance with the heretofore ignored Lieber Code, Sherman had hundreds of heavily armed guards placed all over the town, a relatively wealthy place of around 2,500 inhabitants, to ensure that absolutely no pillaging occurred. Private Job Yaggy of the 124th Illinois Infantry observed this fact in his diary entry of February 27, 1864, a phenomenon of hard discipline which he had not seen at any other time on the Meridian campaign.

> [Canton is] a very nice place 4 churches and a nice large courthouse. It has not been *injured yet* by our troops, guards are all over. The 20th Ills. is under arrest for burning a house.[133]

Why the change of heart by Sherman? In his absence from the army, Sherman did not want any deviations from the law of war in the populous city of Canton so that he could avoid potential criticism should something *unexpected* occur at the tactical or strategic level. If nothing else, this incident absolutely proves not only that Sherman knew how to control his troops, but that he did control them exactly as he wished. When he wanted strict discipline enforced it absolutely happened. When he wanted pillaging and looting to occur that absolutely happened as well. In short, this Southern city was spared the torch of terror and in stark contrast to every other city and town visited by Sherman in his march to and from Meridian nary a single home was looted in "lucky" Canton.

Before dawn on February 28, Sherman trotted out with his escort, the 4th Iowa Cavalry, leaving many in the rank and file greatly perplexed and disappointed with the novel stringent restrictions on ransacking and burning. For instance, Private Alfred Titus wrote a very revealing letter home on March 8, 1864, which confirms two important facts: (1) Sherman always had complete control of his army and it did exactly what he wanted it to do, and (2) arson and pillaging was rampant during the Meridian expedition because Sherman wanted it so.

It seems to me that here is something wrong in this expedition – for [the towns of] Brandon, Morton, Hillsboro, Decatur, and Meridian were burned to the ground – not a building to tell where they stood, the country was very poor, and the inhabitants ditto. I don't believe there were really half a dozen rich men east of the Pearl River – of course – all men [off] in the [Confederate] army as nearly as I could find out .... But as soon as we reached the neighborhood of Canton where the country was rich and the plantations large, where the inhabitants were not only influential and men of wealth but were to a man avowed rebels and told our soldiers so and in some cases the women spit in our boys faces, no sooner had we reached there than Sherman issued an order prohibiting under penalty of being marched to Vicksburg tied behind a wagon with a placard on his back *for the same burning and plundering that heretofore had been encouraged.* Even the wells and cisterns were guarded and we were forced to drink stagnant water enough to make anyone sick [emphasis added].[134]

– Sexual Assault –

As is the downfall with all habitual liars, Sherman would often contradict himself. In his self-serving memoirs written after the War, Sherman actually admits to the fact that war crimes and acts of terror accompanied his troops, although instead of pleading an inability to control his soldiers as he had previously expressed in many contemporary communications to his superiors, he falsely feigned "ignorance" at the time, a position impossible to even consider as truthful particularly given his own telegraphs, remarks, and the many letters to his wife, brother, and others. Sherman wrote in his memoirs:

No doubt, *many acts* of pillage, robbery, and violence, were committed by these parties of foragers, usually called "bummers," for *I have since heard* of jewelry taken from women, and the plunder of articles that never reached the commissary; but these acts were exceptional and incidental. I never heard of any cases of murder or rape ... [emphasis added].[135]

Of course, the discussion of Sherman's culpability regarding the heinous crime of rape must be addressed. In terms of sexual assaults committed by his soldiers, Sherman at first denied that such had ever occurred, but later was forced to correct himself, finally confessing in his own words that he was made aware of:

[A]t least two rapes during the course of the march, and *there were doubtless many more*, as well as widespread theft, intimidation, physical violence, and petty vandalism [emphasis added].[136]

Admittedly, incontrovertible documented cases of sexual assault by Sherman's forces on black and white Southern women and girls are rare in the existing literature, such as the rape of twenty-seven-year-old Kate Nichols in Midway, Georgia, by two Union soldiers. This does not mean, however, that rape was an uncommon crime as Sherman himself admitted and any reasonable mind would conclude given that his soldiers were allowed to do every other act of depredation against innocent civilians. Why would they draw the line at sexual assault?

The reasons that women and girls keep silent are many, not the least involved the societal stigma of being the victim of sexual assault. The social pressures of the day were so strong that most chose to conceal any information about such outrageous violations of their person. Indeed, the Nichols case only came to light because she was subsequently committed to an insane asylum in Milledgeville, Georgia, due to the rape's effect on her mental condition.[137]

Weighing the command directed atmosphere which openly encouraged the brutalization of civilians, it is simply magical thinking to self-righteously assert that torture, rape, and other instances of depravity were unusual occurrences, particularly when one understands that most of these crimes occurred in the countryside on isolated farms where command and control was further limited in scope. The only saving factor for many Southern women was that Sherman moved his troops across Georgia at a relatively fast pace so that even greater degrees of terror were mitigated; Sherman often expressed concern about getting bogged down by the winter weather and intentionally bypassed any Confederate strongpoints such as Augusta (to his north) or Macon (to his south) to avoid such a possibility.

In her extensively researched book on the topic, Yale historian and professor Crystal N. Feimster summed up the overwhelming direct and circumstantial evidence about Union sexual assaults in her important work entitled, *Southern Women and the Politics of Rape and Lynching*:

> Southern women wartime diaries, court martial records, wartime general orders, military reports, and letters written by women, soldiers, doctors, nurses and military chaplains leave little doubt that, as in most wars, rape and the threat of sexual violence figured large in the military campaigns that swept across the Southern landscape.[138]

Another female historian by the name of Jacqueline Glass Campbell, points out that black Southern females were the most vulnerable targets for Union abuse, particularly in Sherman's movement through the South Carolina countryside. She observes that "many [Union] white soldiers viewed black women as a 'legitimate prey of lust.'"[139] Added to the stigma of shame which stifled all victims of rape from reporting these crimes, the issue of "illiteracy and a sense of powerlessness" were certainly key factors pertaining to black females.

> African Americans' reactions to Union soldiers were even more complex. Their initial delight at the coming of the "army of emancipation" was often replaced with terror as Yankees plundered black homes and assaulted black women.[140]

Even if one concedes that these vile acts were not as common as some historians' claim, it is certain that black female Southerners were generally treated far worse than their white counterparts. One Union soldier with Sherman's march observed that it would have been "vexatious to the Grand Turk or to Brigham Young" if either could have seen "how many of the dark houries were in the employment of officers' servants and teamsters."[141] According to one of Sherman's officers many soldiers treated the young black women who fled to the Union ranks for protection as "dark houries" and even provided some with captured horses to ride.[142]

Viewed by many racist Northerners as sub-human, blacks were generally the first to be robbed, abused, and sometimes raped or killed.[143] As but one illustration, a widow named Charlotte Hine recorded that when Union soldiers raided her home in Alabama some of them grabbed her 14-year-old servant, saying, "I want to use you." While two Union soldiers raped the girl, Mrs. Hine helped the mother escape, hearing that she would be next.[144] Another woman, Mary Mallard wrote in her diary entry for December 19, 1864:

> Squads of Yankees [Sherman's cavalry] came all day
> .... These men were so outrageous at the negro houses
> that the negro *men were obliged to stay at their
> houses for the protection of their wives*; and in some
> instances they rescued them from the hands of these
> infamous creatures [emphasis added].[145]

One historian catalogued numerous instances of physical violence and depravity employed by Sherman's men against those Southern blacks that optimistically flocked to the Union for "freedom" – unprovoked shootings, sexual assaults, forced labor, and even drownings.[146] He wrote:

> [I]t was the black refugees who bore the brunt of the
> physical violence, often with little provocation.[147]

During the burning and sacking of Colombia, South Carolina, the streets were filled with drunken Yankees turned loose in the city. No longer shielded by the remoteness of the countryside where their crimes were concealed and hidden from view, eyewitnesses were able to document the unspeakable crimes.

> Federal soldiers raped a number of black women, and one infantryman was killed by an officer while attempting to rape a white girl.[148]

Writing from Columbia, William G. Simms summed up in his diary the matter of Union abuse towards women, apparently something that was the rule and not the exception.

> The shocking details should not now be made, but that we need, for the sake of truth and humanity, to put on record the horrid details. And yet, we should grossly err if, while showing the forbearance of the [Union] soldiers in respect to our white women, we should convey to any innocent reader the notion that they exhibited a like forbearance in the case of the black. The poor negroes were terribly victimized by their assailants, many of them, besides the instance mentioned, being left in a condition little short of death. *Regiments, in successive relays, subjected scores of these poor women to the torture of their embraces*, and – but we dare not further pursue the subject [emphasis added].[149]

While the topic of rape is covered up in many contemporary writings, the case of one such outrage appeared in *History of Sumter County*, and should not be taken as uncommon or an isolated incident.[150]

> A Southern home was invaded by Union troops looking for loot and the owner, a Mr. Robert Bee "was found hanging from the rafters of his attic, tortured and murdered by drunken soldiers, who were said to have raped his daughter," Julia Bee. In Julia's

account, she refuses to mention the rape but does affirm the ransack of the home by a group of Federal troops and that their "faithful servant who was looked upon as one of our household – dear faithful Hannah found looking in the upper rooms, exclaimed as she entered the room – "My God here is my dear Master murdered by the Yankees."[151]

Apart from a handful of Federal court-martial proceedings lodged against a few Union soldiers for war crimes (only one prosecution for the crime of rape is found in the official records), the paucity of letters and diaries that provide details of crimes from the soldiers themselves should not be surprising, particularly of the more horrendous categories of criminal behavior. Criminals rarely record their crimes.

In short, Sherman's policy of terror was intended and he most certainly knew the full range of despicable consequences which would logically follow. Sherman is culpable for his conduct.

Fact: Although Sherman could have easily controlled his army as he had done on previous occasions, he intentionally and with malice aforethought chose not to.

– False Justification Five: Fighting Enemy Armies –

Some defenders of Sherman's blatant crimes in his line of march assert that it was impracticable for him to maintain firm control or to establish a military police force to "watch and discipline his own men because to have done so would have delayed the operation"[152] and opened up his troops to attacks by robust Confederate forces. This contention is totally wrong-headed, but even if true, that a large Confederate army was lurking about in the tall grass ready to pounce on and destroy Sherman at any moment, this factor would still not provide a legal excuse for the utter lawlessness exhibited by his men against innocent civilians.

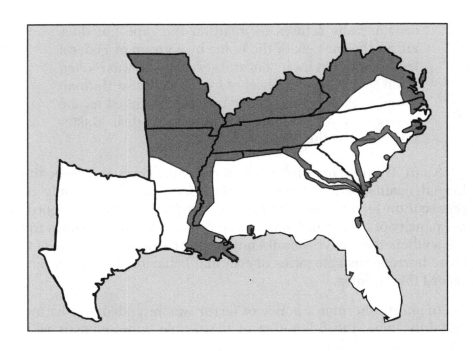

Union Controlled Territory – November 1864 to March 1865.

The truth is that no credible historian has ever asserted that the so-called "brilliant" military operation called the March to the Sea was ever in danger of facing any serious Confederate military opposition. The only significant Confederate force anywhere in the Western Theater at that time to even challenge Sherman was Hood's Army of Tennessee and it was then 300 miles away in Tuscumbia, Alabama, on its way up north into Tennessee.[153] Sherman well knew that only scattered Rebel cavalry under General Joseph Wheeler's depleted division of perhaps 3,500 effectives and a smattering of brave but useless Georgia militia consisting of old men and young boys remained in the operational battle space and represented only token resistance to his massive incursion into Georgia's heartland.

Lincoln's only resignation to the march was a fear that if something did go wrong – unusual weather or disease – it might cause him not to get reelected. Thus, one week after Lincoln was reelected, Sherman started his march and the only nail biting in

Washington were the five weeks of waiting for news of Sherman's success, since all telegraph communications were cut when Sherman left Atlanta on November 15.

Of course, at the core of this line of thinking – that Sherman was only concerned with getting his army quickly across enemy-held Georgia – is the added strange idea that Sherman's great tactical genius and tremendous intellect should somehow mitigate what happened to the innocents.[154] Laughably, Sherman's only grand strategic vision was to terrorize civilians. Even without factoring in his wide spread employment of terrorism against noncombatants, no one can seriously rank the military mind of General Sherman among the brilliant, and certainly never among the noble.

Although Sherman was not immune from lathering on about his supposed military acumen and brilliance, he was always a man of few words about his failures. Most honest post-War observers believe that he was far too cautious when conducting combat operations against sizable concentrations of enemy soldiers – Southern men that could actually defend themselves with weapons.[155] One distinguished military historian correctly summed up Sherman's battlefield skill:

> As a consequence, he tended to hold back both in the employment and deployment of his forces. This in turn either cost him defeats, as at Missionary Ridge, or else lost him the fruits of victory, as at Jonesboro.[156]

Fact: Sherman's imaginary Confederate enemy armies never materialized because they never existed.

– False Justification Six: Lawful Tactics of the Time –

Another popular but erroneous contention by some postmodernist writers is that "General Sherman's march of devastation ... during the American Civil War may have been viewed as lawful tactics at the time."[157] In turn, following World War II several scholars sought to compare violations of the law of war by the United States in that conflict (to include the firebombing of Tokyo), in order to minimize the "total war" tactics of Sherman against civilians.[158]

Such pedestrian thinking is totally at odds with the rock-solid existing law of armed conflict, whether it be the Geneva Conventions in World War II or the firmly encapsulated Lieber Code in Sherman's day. As already seen, the adoption of the Lieber Code as an official military norm for all the Union's armed forces was made absolutely binding by the issuance of General Order 100, particularly so for the officers who were solemnly charged with upholding not only the laws but the necessary good order and discipline attendant to them.[159] The fact that "Union field commanders paid any great attention to General Orders 100 or any similar document,"[160] is irrelevant. It was the law and although it did not contain a self-executing provision, all violations "such as arson, murder, maiming, assaults, highway robbery, theft, burglary, fraud, forgery, and rape" were punishable by the then existing military laws.[161]

While it is true that there was a time in medieval Europe that warfare was waged with the *chevauhee* – militaries on the move systematically pillaged everything and everyone in their path of march – that time had long since passed from the civilized world.[162] Obviously, however, it was brought back to life by the Lincoln Administration as there is no question that Sherman did embrace the full scope of the *chevauhee*, calling it "hard war." It absolutely hinged on terrorizing innocent civilians. As noted already, Sherman spoke with admiration about the "old ways" of European warfare. His theory of terrorism would "compare well with that of the European Models."[163]

Ironically, in twisted arrogance, Sherman made himself believe that his use of raw terror on civilians actually comported with the needs of "civilized warfare." Ten years after the War Sherman unapologetically admitted that his fanciful view of what the rules of armed conflict should be superseded the actual rule of law on the subject. As he told Grant, it was an "Enlightened War,"[164] unencumbered by the Lieber Code. To him, not only was his method of waging war by terror not illegal, it was "civilized!"

> But they [the Confederacy] continued the war, and then we had a right, under the rules of *civilized warfare* to commence a system that would make them feel the power of the government, and cause them to succumb to our national authority [emphasis added].[165]

Sherman's demented vision of "civilized warfare" is the antithesis of civilized behavior. In fact, even before the Union adopted the Lieber Code in 1863, Sherman was openly irritated by the well-established customary law of war prohibitions of the day called the West Point canons. Although Sherman was taught as a cadet at the United States Military Academy to respect the rules protecting civilians,[166] he later "mocked the West Point canons that condemn[ed] atrocities, calling the canons 'old notions.'"[167] Ironically, his justification for terrorism on "inhabitants known or suspected to be hostile or 'secesh'"[168] was also rooted in an open disdain for many of the fundamental guarantees of liberty embodied in the U.S. Constitution and the Declaration of Independence. Sherman called these sacred ideas "trash" and quite naturally bundled them all together as part of a "slave rights" mentality. For example, on January 31, 1864, Sherman wrote the assistant adjutant general of the Army of the Tennessee:

> I am willing to bear in patience that political nonsense of Slave Rights, States Rights, uncontrolled freedom of conscience, License [freedom] of the press, and such other trash as have deluded the Southern People and carried them into War, Anarchy, & blood shed, and the perpetration of some of the foulest of Crimes that have disgraced any time or any people.[169]

Sherman believed that the United States could do as it wished in waging warfare without restriction of law. He proudly offered himself as the chief instrument of such lawlessness, boasting in a long rambling letter to a subordinate stationed at Huntsville, Alabama (he asked his U.S. Senator brother in Ohio to republish the letter in the newspapers) of the need to commit atrocities on the South if the War continued.

The Government of the United States has ... any and all the rights of Sovereignty which they choose to enforce in War, to take their [Southerners] lives, their homes, their lands, their every thing, because they cannot deny that War does exist by their acts, and War is simply Power unrestrained by Constitution or Compact.[170]

Put in another way, Sherman's general thought pattern seemed to justify his disregard for the rules of warfare by claiming that because war is by nature harsh, one need not abide by the rules designed to mitigate the horror. In a long letter to the mayor of Atlanta, John Calhoun, Sherman rejected outright any pleas for treating civilian noncombatants with humanity.

You cannot qualify war in harsher terms than I will. War is cruelty and you cannot refine it those who brought war into our country deserve all the curses and maledictions a people can pour out .... You might as well appeal against the thunderstorm as against these terrible hardships of war [targeting civilians with terror].[171]

Of course, this cynical view of the rule of law is as old as it is fallacious.[172] The statement by Rome's Marcus Tullius Cicero (106-43 B.C.) *"inter arma legis silent,"* which means, "in war the law is silent," was not true in the time of Rome and was not true during Sherman's tenure in the United States military. Even two thousand years ago, the Roman military had very specific laws on the regulation of hostilities as did the armed forces of the United States and the Confederate States. Specific rules regulating the conduct of warfare and the associated punishments for those who violated those rules have always existed from the beginning of recorded history. One of the earliest examples of rules regulating combat to mitigate civilian suffering comes from the *Torah*. For example, in the book of *Deuteronomy,* the Hebrews were given specific instructions on the protections that were to be afforded to the inhabitants of a city under siege. In all cases, torture was prohibited. Similarly, fruit trees outside of a besieged city were protected from destruction; the fruit could be eaten, but it was unlawful to cut down the tree.[173]

To summarize, to assert that Sherman's tactics were lawful suggests a gross ignorance or out and out denial of the legal authority of the Lieber Code. Only an audience predisposed to covering up the atrocities, where the winners write the history books as they wish regardless of the facts, would even entertain such an absurd proposition.

After the War, South Carolinian Daniel Heyward recorded a conversation he had with General Lee concerning Sherman's wholesale burning of civilian homes in South Carolina as measured by the law of war.

> I called on General Lee in Savannah, when on the way to Florida to restore his broken health .... I asked: "Was General Sherman justified, under the usages of war, in burning as he passed through South Carolina, the homes of our women and children while our men were in the field, fighting him bravely?" His eye flashed as on the battlefield, and half rising from his seat, he said in a voice more emphatic than I ever heard him: "No sir! No, sir! *It was the act of a savage, and not justified by the usages of war* [emphasis added]."[174]

Fact: The Lieber Code and the customary international law of war absolutely prohibited Sherman's war crimes and terrorism.

– False Justification Seven: Command Responsibility –

The concept of command responsibility refers to the long-standing rule of law that the commander of a military organization is legally responsible for the illegal use of force taken by those under his authority/command. For the commander, this is expressed in two areas of concern – "direct responsibility" and "indirect responsibility." In other words, even though the commander himself does not physically commit the violations of the law of war, if he orders the illegal acts, he is directly responsible for those crimes. In turn, under indirect responsibility, if the commander knows of ongoing violations of the law of war committed by his soldiers and does nothing to stop them, he too is guilty of those crimes.

Legal applications of direct and indirect command responsibility are illustrated from two American war crimes trails. The most egregious norm to apply to a commander is the "direct knowledge" standard, where a commander intentionally orders his men to engage in a violation of the law of war and the violation occurs. He is guilty of all those crimes. Although this truth has existed for centuries, it is known as the *Medina* standard in American jurisprudence, so named from the court-martial of Captain Ernest Medina for his direct role in ordering men under his command to murder hundreds of civilians at the My Lai massacre in Vietnam.[175]

The second standard for command culpability, indirect responsibility, comes out of the Yamashita war crimes trial from World War II. Yamashita, a Japanese general officer, was tried and convicted for the rape and murder spree committed by 20,000 Japanese troops in Manila, Philippines during 1945.[176] Although the military commission was unable to prove that Yamashita directly ordered the atrocities, it rightly held him responsible under a "should have known" theory. Under this application of indirect responsibility, if, through normal events, the commander *should have known* of the crimes, but did nothing to stop his soldiers, he is guilty of the actions of his soldiers. However, the *Yamashita* should have known standard of indirect responsibility applies only when there is a widespread pattern of abuse over a prolonged period of time. In such a scenario, the commander is presumed either to have knowledge of the crimes or, if he actually has no knowledge, to have abandoned his command. This certainly fits Sherman's march across Georgia and South Carolina. As one historian correctly put it:

> Sherman knew, or should have known, that his men would leave devastation and misery in their wake, giving rise to charges of cruelty and barbarism.[177]

There is no question that General Sherman bears both "direct responsibility" and "indirect responsibility" for the unchecked spiral of terror committed by his own soldiers. That the terrorism occurred over a prolonged period of time and was widespread is without debate. Similarly, that Sherman actually knew that terrorism had occurred, was occurring, and would occur is without debate – it all happened right under his nose as he rode along with his army. While Sherman's Order 120 does not specifically order the depredations, pillaging, and burning, only the *non compos mentis* would assert that he did not directly intend for the war crimes to occur. His own words to his friends and superiors at the time convict him. There is no doubt that he "believed himself justified in ending it [the War] by any means short of outright genocide."[178] As but one of his many acknowledgements of what his violations of the law of war produced even prior to his march across Georgia, Sherman wrote:

> We have devoured the land and our animals eat up the wheat and cornfields close. All the people retire before us and desolation is behind. To realize what war is one should follow our tracks.[179]

One of the highest-ranking Union officers was General Henry Halleck, who was also a scholar of the law of war. As the commander in the Western Theater of conflict prior to Grant's tenure there, he was careful to abide by the long-established international rules of warfare. A pragmatist, Halleck realized that war crimes were bound to occur by individual soldiers acting outside of the law, but understood that it was the commander who was responsible to set the tone and control his soldiers so that such outrages were the exception and not the rule. He wrote:

> It is true that soldiers sometimes commit excesses which their officers cannot prevent; but, in general, a commanding officer is responsible for the acts of those under his command. Unless he can control his soldiers, he is unfit to command them.[180]

In Sherman's case, either avenue, direct or indirect responsibility, the crimes were command approved and warranted his immediate dismissal from command and the attendant just punishments for the horrendous abuses that occurred on his watch. Also, included on the long list of senior Union generals who directly or indirectly breached the law of armed conflict under the Lieber Code *vis a vis* civilians would be General Phillip Sheridan and General "Black Dave" Hunter in the Shenandoah Valley (the nickname for his burning of civilian homes).

In addition, Sherman, Sheridan, or Hunter could not rely on the defense of "superior orders" from General Grant or Abraham Lincoln to escape responsibility – even though both were sly enough to disavow and distance themselves from directly issuing such orders to their subordinates. This particular legal norm was firmly established in the context of the only significant war crimes criminal trial that came out of the War – the Union military court-martial of Confederate Major Henry Wirz. Major Wirz was the commandant of the notorious Andersonville prisoner of war camp in Georgia and was charged by the United States with numerous offenses, to include murder. Although the evidence portion of the trial was horribly flawed in many respects, it correctly affirmed a principle of law that violations of the law of war were inexcusable and the defense of superior orders could not remove the guilt of the accused.[181] Major Wirz was not convicted of personally killing any single prisoner of war, but under the "should have known" standard he was convicted of murder and subsequently executed.

– Lincoln Knew –

Understandably, Sherman's conduct was evidently not so shocking to the Lincoln Administration or members of Congress.[182] As previously discussed, although Lincoln never specifically authorized the scorched-earth terror policy in writing, he knew all about it and did nothing. Although camouflaging the matter of the terror policy targeting civilians with the phrase "Confederate resources," one historian correctly noted:

> What Lincoln authorized, and men like Sherman carried out, was a plan to exhaust Confederate resources [civilian terror tactics] and destroy civilian morale.[183]

As covered in Chapter Three, Lincoln knew what was happening; he completely condoned the crimes. Thus, it is understandable that neither Sherman nor any of the other senior Union generals that

Lincoln in the field with Gen. McClellan, Sharpsburg, Maryland, 1862.

conducted terror tactics in the 1864-1865 time frame ever faced disciplinary action, sanction, or even admonition from Washington, meaning that the Commander in Chief consciously and freely accepted these outrages. Ever the micro-manager of all things that occurred in the conduct of the War – he would anxiously consume any news or rumor and spent hours perched at the Washington telegraph center for the latest news from the field – it is impossible to contend anything other than the fact that Lincoln knew exactly what was happening under the Union's scorched-earth policy of terrorism against innocent civilians. Sherman himself knew that Lincoln, Grant, and Stanton approved of his terrorism. For instance, after occupying Atlanta, Sherman wrote General Halleck in September 1864:

> I wish you would thank the President and Secretary [the Secretary of War, Stanton] for the *constant support* they have given me, and accept from me my personal assurance that I have always felt more buoyed up by the knowledge that you were there [emphasis added].[184]

Most certainly, though, Lincoln generally hoped to avoid personal responsibility by simply remaining silent on the war crimes, or even duplicitously voicing opposition to them in the occasional public statement he might make on the topic. Then again, to those who study the dark side of Lincoln, this was the same man who jailed 36,000 *Northern* citizens for daring to speak or write against his administration. It was also the Lincoln Administration that condoned the forced evacuation of every human being in most of the border areas of western Missouri and, pursuant to General Order Number 11, approved of the burning of every single civilian home – 20,000 dwellings.[185]

Those defenders of Lincoln expose an intellectual bankruptcy when they assert that he had no idea of the barbaric and cruel destruction that his generals were conducting. As historian Thomas J. DiLorenzo correctly observes:

> One cannot praise Lincoln for his pervasive intervention in war management on the one hand, while on the other hand claiming that he had no idea what was occurring [terrorism on civilians] on a massive scale for years.[186]

Many attribute the "giving a pass" attitude towards Lincoln to "Lincoln worship," a phenomenon which became extremely powerful after his death. Accordingly, commentators rarely criticize him or his polices and read into his personal life history a plethora of progressive and social ideals that he never held or championed himself. One commentator once quipped that "Lincoln was the only person he knew that became a Christian after he died."[187] Despite the fact that President Lincoln had a penchant for referring to "Almighty God" in public speeches, there is no evidence in any of his writings that he believed in Jesus Christ as his Savior.[188] At most his wife simply called him a "poetic Christian" after his death.

In addition, Sherman's direct superior General Grant also shares culpability for Sherman's actions. Like Lincoln, it is a matter of record that Grant never addressed Sherman's many dark communiqués where Sherman expressed a sense of rapture about the suffering inflicted by his men on Southern civilians. On the contrary, Grant actually approved of, and later defended, the barbarous actions of his favorite subordinate.[189] That Lincoln and Grant rubber stamped the horrid use of terrorism should be disturbing, but not surprising. The bottom line is undeniable. There is simply no question that Lincoln and Grant approved of Sherman's conduct and even pro-Union books are forced to admit it, but without condemnation. For example:

> Sherman and 62,000 Union troops set out for Savannah, George, burning homes, pillaging plantations, and taking livestock along the way. His goal – *approved by Abraham Lincoln* – was to convince civilians to give up the Confederate cause. "I can make Georgia howl"! he telegraphed Grant [emphasis added].[190]

At the end of the day the ultimate person responsible for the Union's abuse of power and use of terrorism is rolled up into one person – Abraham Lincoln. As the Commander in Chief, it was his responsibility to enforce legality and morality and do all he could to wage war under the rule of law and not the rule of the jungle.

– Cover Your Behind (CYA) –

Nevertheless, not all Union generals acquiesced to the illegal use of terror on civilians. To be accurate, it is certainly true that some of Sherman's subordinate officers understood the legal issue of command responsibility and the attendant consequences. While none of them resigned their commissions or posts in protest, there is a great deal of real time correspondence that can best be described as guilty "hand wringing" by leaders under Sherman's command who felt otherwise obligated to abide by the provisions of General Order 100 and to maintain the required level of military discipline to control the men under their charge. Much of this was to no use, however, particularly when Sherman's troops discovered that little real effort was made to protect civilians or civilian property.

For instance, early in the march across Georgia, Major General Oliver Howard dutifully informed Sherman that the soldiers were committing "inexcusable and wanton acts" against civilians in direct violation of Sherman's "orders."[191] Then, when Howard discerned that Sherman was in no way serious about enforcing the orders to stop the crimes he quickly followed his boss' lead and issued similar orders to his own subordinate corps officers outlawing the terror tactics of arson and robbery, but only to also shield himself from future accusations of complicity in the war crimes should the truth emerge. General Howard uselessly ordered:

> It having come to the knowledge of the major general [General Howard] commanding that the crime of arson and robbery have become frequent throughout this army, notwithstanding positive orders both from these and superior headquarters having been repeatedly issued ... it is hereby ordered: that Hereinafter any officer or man of this command discovered in *pillaging a house or burning a building* without proper authority, will upon sufficient proof thereof, *be shot* [emphasis added].[192]

Despite such "official" imprecations by Union commanders like Howard that threatened death by firing squad for any form of pillaging, not a single Union soldier was ever executed and only a handful caught in the act of the most despicable felony crimes were ever prosecuted. Those few miscreants that were convicted were given ridiculously reduced sentences, many returning right back to the ranks.[193] Like his superior Sherman, General Howard made sure to protect his name and cover his own *gluteus maximus*; the obligatory official outrage was given for the historical record. As one historian understated:

> [H]is men knew he [Sherman] would *understand* if they went beyond the orders. A great deal of unauthorized and individual looting went on as the army ripped across the state [Georgia], and it went *unpunished* [emphasis added].[194]

Other subordinate officers started out as otherwise honorable men, but became morally corrupted under the influence and atmosphere of Sherman's leadership. Major James Connolly, who served under Sherman on his terror rampage through Georgia and South Carolina, was a direct eyewitness and recorder of many of the atrocities. Connolly was at first repulsed by the blue clad soldiers who went to work with an orgy of depredations, but then, shielded by a true understanding of Sherman's policy, he learned to turn a callous heart towards it all as things proceeded. Notwithstanding the fact that the women and children of the South faced brutality while their counterparts in the North remained sheltered, Connolly ultimately elected to mimic Sherman's barbarism. He wrote:

> We'll *burn every house, barn, church*, and everything
> else we come to; *we'll leave their families houseless
> and without food*; their towns will all be destroyed,
> and nothing but the most complete desolation will be
> found in our track [emphasis added].[195]

Fact: The core requirements of command responsibility were violated and Sherman is guilty of direct and indirect war crimes which were carried out by his own soldiers.

– False Justification Eight: End Justifies the Means –

The final false justification – the end justifies the means – is perhaps the most insidious to the rule of law and core human decency. At its center, this fallacious argument rests squarely in the realm of "situational ethics" and rejects the existence of intrinsic truth as unambiguously revealed in the Christian Bible. Citing with approval the so-called utilitarian principle of morality, best developed by philosopher Jeremy Bentham, proponents of the end the justifies the means excuse for Union terror equate to "the blind leading the blind."

There are a great number of words in the English language to describe a person who not only does the *right thing* in a given situation, but performs that action in the *right way*. Such a person may be described as exhibiting virtue, integrity, honor, and courage.

Without question, the formula of doing a right thing in a right way is an essential ingredient for the establishment and development of a just and democratic society based on the rule of law. Conversely, deviations from the formula are destructive to the individual and to the society he resides in. For instance, it is a right thing to acquire food, but stealing to accomplish this goal can only be characterized as wrong. Thus, doing a right thing, eating, must be done in a right way, by paying for the food, or the result is wrong. No excuses, no false justifications.

The absurd narrative that Union sponsored terrorism was justified is summed up with unflinching approval by W. Todd Groce, President and Chief Executive of the Georgia Historical Society. She wrote: "Sherman demonstrated for the first time in the modern era the power of terror and psychological warfare in breaking an enemy."[196] Reflecting Groce's viewpoint, claiming that his barbarous use of terror had a bright side, that is, it would induce Southern civilians to sue for peace, Sherman himself freely admitted his intent to terrorize civilians and blamed anyone but himself for the crimes.

> If they [civilians in the South] raise a *howl* against my *barbarity* and *cruelty*, I will answer that war is war, and not popularity-seeking. If they want peace, they and their relatives must stop the war [emphasis added].[197]

Tragically, the only persons who "howl" under such brutal activities are members of the defenseless civilian population. Sherman, however, did not care because under the misguided theory of *consequentialism* the consequences of one's own conduct are all that matters, not the "rightness" or "wrongness" of the conduct. In other words, vicious methods may be used in warfare if the overall results of that come out of the atrocities are deemed *good*. Of course, such is utter nonsense. In the light of situational ethics there are no rules and each of the opposing parties can play the game of consequentialism to justify any and every foul deed committed. Both sides can simply claim that their cause is just and good and instead of being appalled by their minions who commit war crimes and terror, heap accolades on them.

Because most of modern America swallows the simplistic narrative that the virtuous North fought the Civil War in order to "free the slaves," the Union's employment of widespread terrorism against civilians is ignored or brushed aside as a necessary evil to achieve the ultimate good. Not only is this narrative a revisionist view of American history, it demonstrates a phenomenal lack of critical thinking skills. While most Americans at the time of the Civil War, North and South, would agree that slavery was a moral wrong, the United States most certainly did not invade the Confederate States for the purpose of the manumission of slaves. Indeed, throughout the entire war the two belligerent nations were both "slave holding countries."

Like most Americans in antebellum America — to include slave owner President Thomas Jefferson — Lincoln's personal view was that "all men should be free," but his decision for attacking the eleven Southern States that had lawfully chosen to leave the United States in peace was solely to force them back into the Union, not to abolish slavery. Indeed, when Lincoln did issue his wartime Emancipation Proclamation it did not free slaves in the United States, only in the Confederate States that were then in "rebellion." Slavery was not abolished in the Union States of Maryland, Kentucky, Delaware, and Missouri until well after the Civil War, with the passage of the 13th Amendment to the Constitution in December 1865. In 1862, the *New York Times* published perhaps Lincoln's most famous letter describing in detail his motivation for using armed violence against the Confederacy.

> My paramount object in this struggle is to save the Union, and is not either to save or to destroy slavery. If I could save the Union without freeing any slave I would do it, and if I could save it by freeing all the slaves I would do it; and if I could save it by freeing some and leaving others alone I would also do that. What I do about slavery, and the colored race, I do because I believe it helps to save the Union; and what I forbear, I forbear because I do not believe it would help to save the Union. I shall do less whenever I

shall believe what I am doing hurts the cause, and
I shall do more whenever I shall believe doing more
will help the cause.[198]

Interestingly, the spirit of preserving the Union was only energized to action by the Confederacy's monumental blunder in firing cannons on Fort Sumter on April 12, 1861, when goaded by the Lincoln Administration to do so. It was a brilliant move by Lincoln to activate his use of armed force – the propaganda that the South had started the War transformed an ambivalent United States into a solid block behind Lincoln's plan to invade.

The powerful mantra to save or preserve the Union is perfectly illustrated in a 1861 letter penned by Union Major Sullivan Ballou to his beloved wife on the night before he was mortally wounded at First Manassas. Ballou reminded his wife about the heroes of the American Revolution who had given so much to establish the United States as a country and the heavy debt all Americans owed them to keep it intact. He wrote: "And I am willing – perfectly willing – to lay down all my joys in this life, to help maintain this Government and to pay that debt."[199]

In tandem with Lincoln and the majority of Northerners, Sherman never asserted that he was fighting to free enslaved people. His terror tactics were always about punishing Southerners for departing from the Union to the point that they would repent and cease resisting the armies sent to suppress the Confederacy.

Accordingly, there is no question that Sherman excluded himself from the restrictions imposed by the law of armed conflict in order to engage in terror tactics against civilians under the old saw that the "end justifies the means." For instance, in his rambling and incoherent response to the mayor of Atlanta regarding his treatment of battered Southern civilians after the Federals took the city, Sherman openly admitted that he disregarded Article 16 both in spirit and in letter because, in his mind, the horrendous terror tactics would cause the Southern people to give up their quest for independence.

We don't want your Negroes, your horses, or your house, or your land, or anything you have, but we do want and will have first obedience to the laws of the United States ... if it involves the destruction of your *improvements*, we cannot help it [emphasis added].[200]

– An Avenging Angel of Suffering –

Rubricated by a manic depressive personality, which peers, family and attending physicians described as paranoid delusions, General Sherman was perfectly suited to execute the grotesque orgy of real and psychological terrorism on civilians. Even the friendliest biographer of William T. Sherman concedes that he was haunted by a plethora of personal demons and by this stage of the War the wild-eyed miscreant had convinced himself that command directed terror against women and children was completely justified. In what the modern psychologist would deem a severe case of "projection" – placing one's own deficiencies and flaws onto others – Sherman took to long tirades railing against the people of the South, bizarrely accusing them of the "foulest crimes that have disgraced any time or any people."[201] As it turned out, his uncontrollable rants were nothing more than a revealing description of himself and his disgraceful propensity for committing *the foulest crimes that have disgraced any time or any people.* In sum, his words described himself!

The scale of marauding and vandalism he inflicted on the elderly, women, and children was methodical and intentional, requiring Sherman to thoroughly psyche himself out to the point that inflicting raw suffering on Southerners who refused to "repent" was somehow a just, holy, and deserved penalty. Sherman loathed the people of the Confederacy and on more than one occasion the gaunt and unkempt Ohioan described himself as an "avenging angel" from God who would bring death and destruction to "the petulant and persistent secessionists ... he or she."[202]

In Sherman's twisted thinking all Southerners were legitimate targets of terror and suffering. In his many public comments on the matter he often buttressed his position with the end justifies the means argument. In other words, his goal in using terror was not only to get the Southern people to stop supporting the Confederate government, but to make them *suffer* for daring to have left the Union in the first place. Sherman plainly admitted to the dual purpose of his terror tactics in a post-war speech delivered in Columbus, Ohio, in 1880:

> My aim was to whip the rebels, to humble their pride, to follow them to their inmost recesses [their homes], and *make them fear and dread us* [emphasis added].[203]

The truth is that Sherman took great pleasure and spite in causing pain and suffering on women and children simply for the sake of punishment. Freely admitting that he reserved his worst for the people of South Carolina, Sherman confided to a group of officers at the admiral's quarters in Savannah:

> When I go through South Carolina, it will be one of the most horrible things in the history of the world. The devil himself could not restrain my men in that state."[204]

Because South Carolina was the first Southern State to secede from the Union, Sherman felt that the citizens of that State should be made to suffer the most. Georgia had most certainly burned as he intended, and Sherman proudly bragged to the same group of officers about how thrilled it made him feel when he could "look forty miles in each direction and see smoke rolling up like one great bonfire;"[205] but he would save his best terror for South Carolina.

Indeed, Sherman kept his word and thoroughly devastated the homes and lives of those South Carolinian civilians that had the tragic misfortune of living in his line of advance. An internationally recognized novelist, poet, and historian, William Gilmore Simms traveled through South Carolina in Sherman's wake and faithfully recorded the heart-breaking sights that greeted him.

No language can describe, nor can catalogue furnish, an adequate detail of the wide-spread destruction of homes and property. Granaries were emptied, and where the grain was not carried off, it was strewn to waste under the feet of the cavalry or consigned to the fire which consumed the dwelling. The negroes were robbed equally with the whites of food and clothing. The roads were covered with butchered cattle, hogs, mules, and the costliest furniture.... The inhabitants, black no less than whites, were left to starve, compelled to feed only upon the garbage to be found in the abandoned camps of the [Union] soldiers. The corn scraped up from the spots where the horses fed, has been the only means of life left to thousands but lately in affluence.[206]

Henry D. Jenkins, a former enslaved American from South Carolina summed it up best when he wrote:

[Everything] was took and carried away by an army that seemed more concerned about stealing, than they was about the Holy War for the liberation of the poor African slave people. They took off all the horses, sheeps, cows, chickens, and geese, took the seine [swine] and the fishes they caught, corn in crib, meat in smoke house, and everything. *Master General Sherman said war was hell. It sure was.* Maybe it was hell for some of them Yankees when they come to die and give account of the deeds they done in Sumter and Richland Counties [emphasis added].[207]

– Drinking the Kool-Aid –

Amazingly, apologists for the brutality and terror wrought by Sherman can count in their membership even so-called "conservative" thinkers, such as Hoover Institute's Victor Davis Hanson, who is quick to describe the despicable Union terror tactics in his book, *The Soul of Battle: From Ancient Times to the Present*

Day, How Three Liberators Vanquished Tyranny, but nevertheless lauds Sherman as a great liberator![208] Much like Harvard Law School former Dean Alan Dershowitz's flawed argument that the use of torture can be justified against certain detainees suspected of terrorism[209] regardless of the strict rule law set out in the Torture Convention[210] which absolutely outlaws the use of torture under any circumstances, Hanson is equally wrong-headed in his approval of Sherman's use of terror against civilians.[211]

As, Article 2 of the Torture Convention absolutely prohibits any end justifies the means excuses for engaging in the tactic of torture, so too does the Lieber Code for brutalizing civilians.

> No exceptional circumstances whatsoever, whether a state of war or a threat of war, internal political instability or any other public emergency, may be invoked as a justification for torture.[212]

Finally, some defenders of the Union's use of terror seek to raise the long standing English common law doctrine of "necessity" to excuse or mitigate the wrongs. The necessity doctrine is a very narrow legal justification defense for a criminal defendant who seeks to avoid criminality for his actions by arguing to the Court that he acted in an emergency that he did not create and who committed a harm that was less severe than the harm that would have occurred but for his immediate actions. American law professor Wayne LaFave's amplifies this definition by explaining that "the harm done is justified by the fact that the action taken either accomplished a greater good or prevented a greater harm."[213] In other words, the criminal defendant admits that he did an evil/wrong, but only in order to prevent a greater evil/wrong.

The general understanding of the necessity defense at English common law and during the time period of the 19th Century was that it was in response to circumstances emanating from the physical forces of nature and not from people. For example, a criminal defendant on trial for destroying a home by flooding the structure might argue that he intentionally opened up a dam to release excess water which then destroyed the single home in the path of that water, but did so in order to keep the dam itself from bursting which would have washed away an entire town. Although in the modern era the distinction between the pressure coming from nature or human beings has merged, the necessity defense would not apply as a legal shield for the Union, as either a general or specific defense, due to that fact that the use of terror was a *national policy* of terror. The necessity defense is available for individual defendants facing criminal proceedings, not nations. Nevertheless, it is efficacious to examine the accompanying doctrinal elements which the criminal defendant must satisfy.

Again, proponents of the defense of necessity to excuse the Union's criminal use of terrorism would argue that the greater wrong/evil in the overarching legal formula was the institution of slavery itself. The lesser wrong/evil would be the Union's illegal use of terrorism in violation of the Lieber Code.

First, the criminal defendant must reasonably believe that there was an actual wrong that demanded immediate action. While all can agree that slavery was an evil and a wrong, given that the Union still maintained the institution of slavery within its own territory throughout the entire War, this element is most certainly not met.

Second, the criminal defendant must have no viable alternative to his criminal conduct, in this case the use of wanton terror on civilians. Given that the Union enjoyed a vastly superior military force and was clearly winning the War on the battlefield by 1864, when Union terror reached its peak, the realistic and viable alternative to terrorizing the innocents was to continue the use of lawful combat against the armed forces of the Confederacy to subdue Richmond.

Third, the harm caused by the criminal conduct of the defendant must not be greater than the harm avoided. Given the widespread and prolonged use of terrorism on innocent civilians – black and white Southerners – this prong is not satisfied.

Fourth, the criminal defendant did not cause or contribute to the perceived threat. Again, if the perceived threat is the institution of slavery existing in the United States, the Union is guilty of not only profiting off of the institution for years and years but dragging its feet to end it.

Interestingly, the argument to prop up the defense of necessity on such a grand scale would require one to chart a legal course around the protections of the United States Constitution, while simultaneously ignoring the binding obligations of the law of war. Adding to the fact that although common domestic criminal law may recognize the defense of necessity in certain limited circumstances, the law of war absolutely does not. Indeed, the law of war was designed to protect innocent civilians, not terrorize and brutalize them. Willfully causing great suffering or serious injury to body or health and extensive destruction and appropriation of property, not justified by military necessity and carried out unlawfully and wantonly against persons or property protected by the Lieber Code, is criminal and without defense. Deliberate attacks on noncombatant civilians clearly violates the codified and customary laws of war.

In this light, the sanctioned use of terrorism must surely strike the vast majority as inconsistent with civilized values. Those who believe that the Union properly defended freedom by grossly subverting its own moral and legal values are as misguided as those who demand that the government must fight any war without altering civil liberties by jot or tittle. Of course some restrictions on liberty and freedom will occur in wartime but this line of reasoning does not encompass barbarism.

No one can disagree that the rule of law and democracy are cherished values that must be protected and that in time of war it is sometimes necessary to, as Abraham Lincoln advocated, "suspend our liberties to protect our liberties." In fact, Lincoln denied habeas corpus and unilaterally jailed thousands of American citizens (in the North) who expressed dissent.

In other words, no excuse, real or imagined, can justify the premeditated use of either terrorism or torture. Both are violations of the rule of law – the Lieber Code in Sherman's day and the

Torture Convention in the modern era. Commentators who applaud Sherman as a hero for committing war crimes and terror are not only exhibiting flawed thinking but they actually reveal to the serious student more about our current times, where the masses are content to drink deeply from the waters of political correctness, than the historic period that they ostensibly seek to describe. The ease in which many sugar-coat over the horrid atrocities of Union terror is a stunning condemnation of the society in which Americans now live. The moral code of a civilized people must not tolerate such absurdity.

At no time did the Confederacy stoop to the barbarism of terrorism of terrorism against Union civilians. In fact, perhaps the most bitter irony of all is that Lincoln's often quoted Gettysburg address – "that a government of the people, by the people, and for the people, shall not perish from the earth"[214] – precisely defined the principle for which the South was defending itself. In other words, how can a war waged for a government "of the people" require that many of those people be forced at gunpoint to "consent" to it? Consent cannot be obtained by the barrel of a gun! There is no virtue in this approach to life and liberty.

Fact: To a civilized people, no "end justifies the means" excuse can ever hold water – intellectually, morally, or legally.

Chapter Six

Did Union Terror Work?

"Conceding to our enemies the superiority claimed by them of numbers, resources and all the means and appliances for carrying on the war, we have no right to look for exemptions from the military consequences of a vigorous use of these advantages."[215] *– Robert E. Lee*

THE SHORT ANSWER to the question of whether the Union's use of terror significantly contributed to the end of the conflict is no. No, it did not. As pointed out in Chapter Five, many commentators and others simply view the use of Union terrorism as a necessary evil to achieve a desired goal and are quick to stick their heads in the sand when confronted with the attendant legal and moral objections. However, given that the widespread pattern of gross violations of the law of war by Union forces were designed to demoralize the South and speed along an end to the conflict, one has to ask two overlapping questions: Was it really necessary? Did it work?

The contention that Union violations of the law of war were necessary in an end justifies the means analysis – the most popular of the false justifications – is fundamentally inaccurate for several reasons. First, aside from the obvious issues of morality and casting aside of the rule of law, violations are an unwise waste of military resources. As the pragmatic Prussian soldier and author, Karl von Clausewitz, observed:

If we find civilized nations do not ... devastate towns and countries, this is because their intelligence exercises greater influence on their mode of carrying on War, and has taught them a more effectual means of applying force.[216]

Second, and more importantly, command directed atrocities create a hindrance to a restoration of peace once the War is over. Only two days into Sherman's march of terror from Atlanta to Savannah, at least one Union officer pondered that very matter.

In what way will the destruction of so much [civilian] property aid us in restoring peace, harmony and union in our distracted country?[217]

Third, although the havoc wreaked by Sherman's hordes to "starve out" the people may have contributed to the Confederate defeat, this contribution was so indirect and ambiguous that it did not justify militarily, much less morally, the human misery that accompanied it.[218] In point of fact, the atrocities actually had the opposite effect. As Sherman's plundering grew in scope most women of the South exhorted their men to remain with their armies in the field, particularly Robert E. Lee's Army of Northern Virginia. The people would support the nation. A North Carolinian woman who suffered the destruction of her home by pillaging Yankees was mocked by them asking her what she would "live upon now?" Her answer was echoed by countless Southerners:

[I will live] upon patriotism: I will exist upon the love of my country as long as it will last, and then I will die as firm in that love as the everlasting hills.[219]

Sherman approved of it all and saw with his own eyes what his terror tactics wrought. Still, he admitted on several occasion that he was greatly puzzled that the women and children still resisted. He wrote to his wife:

I doubt if history affords a parallel to the deep and bitter enmity of the women of the South. No one who sees them and hears them but must feel the intensity of their hate. Not a man is seen; nothing but women with houses plundered ... *begging with one breath for a soldiers' rations* and in another praying that the Almighty or Joe Johnston will come and kill us, the *despoilers of their homes and all that is sacred* [emphasis added].[220]

In fact, Sherman was early on baffled by the realization that the scorched-earth policy he had practiced so wholeheartedly in the Meridian campaign had not worked out as intended. Sounding like a psychopathic malefactor, he confided to his wife in a March 1864, letter:

The devils [Southerners] seem to have a determination that cannot but be admired. No amount of poverty or adversity seems to shake their faith – niggers gone – wealth and luxury gone, money worthless, starvation in view within a period of two or three years, are causes enough to make the bravest tremble, yet I see no sign of let up – some few deserters – plenty tired of war, but the masses determined to fight it out.[221]

Mayor Hitchcock recorded the same phenomenon during the March to the Sea when he observed that despite being subjected to waves of terrorism that the defenseless women remained absolutely defiant. "I must say they show little fear of us."[222] Indeed, the women fought back with the only weapon they had – an unconquerable spirit. One Southern woman who watched helplessly as her farm was devastated by marauding Yankees shrieked out to them in hot defiance:

Our men will fight you as long as they live and these boys [the children by her side] will fight you when they grow up.[223]

A young servant girl named Tabitha expressed similar outrage when Yankee soldiers ransacked her quarters and stole dresses and hats. Shaking her fists, she shouted, "Oh! If I had the power like I've got the will, I'd tear you to pieces."[224] Along with thousands of black Southern refugees, whatever positive expectations she had about the Union cause were most certainly diminished.

The true conclusion is that Sherman's unbridled atrocities simply sowed the seeds of hatred for subsequent generations of Southerners – a common epitaph for those who commit war crimes. His assumption that he could terrorize the Confederacy into submission by devastating their livelihood, farms, and towns turned out to be fallacious, as Sherman himself had to admit.

In summation, the conventional wisdom espoused from the sheltered confines of academic dialogue that scorched-earth Union atrocities caused the level of demoralization and disaffection in the civilian population to topple the Confederacy is grossly exaggerated. On the contrary, the truth of the matter is that the wide-spread terror crimes only stiffened resistance to the invaders. Stalwart people cannot be terrorized into submission.

– Why the South Lost –

The "Lost Cause"[225] interpretation of why the South failed to gain its independence is firmly rooted in large measure to the disparity of resources between the Confederacy and the Union. The basic tenants of this calculation are too solidly rooted in fact to be ridiculed, the North possessed more soldiers, more supplies, more money, more machines of war, and more of everything else except courage. But to this imbalance of resources must also be added the poor strategic decisions of the Confederate high command in Richmond to meet the Union invasion of their country.

Bending in part to the normal needs from individual States in the Confederacy, but also as a result of the doctrine of States rights itself, Confederate President Jefferson Davis' survival policy for the nascent nation was to spread his limited military resources across the entire

South to defend it at any given point from Federal invasion. He called this grand plan one of "static defense." However, instead setting up strong concentrations of soldiers at key geographic strategic points, Davis scattered scarce resources across the entire land.[226] Accordingly, the Southern Confederacy was divided into eight semi-independent geographic departments with the hope that working on interior lines, men and material could shift from one area to another as the need arose. While this strategy would bear some tactical fruit at such battles as First Manassas (1861) and Chickamauga (1863), there were powerful contravening factors working against it. Not only were the scarce and non-standard publicly owned Southern railway systems not up to the task of shifting forces about in a timely manner across hundreds of miles of territory, but time and again Richmond was stymied by the selfishness of individual States within the Confederacy which too often hoarded men and supplies for perceived intrastate needs, real and imagined.

At the end of the day, even though the Southern armies won more battles than not, the vast superiority of the United States in terms of manpower and supplies would ultimately prove fatal given the Confederacy's ever dwindling limited resources and lack of a strong centralized government. In many ways, the War was a repeat of the situation in 1776, when the 13 independent Colonies fought their own mother country for the right to form a new nation – David fighting Goliath. While many felt that the only real hope for survival was to simply continue a protracted defense and that by winning enough battles here and there that the United States would grow weary and stop the invasion, others argued that the better path was for an aggressive military strike into the North where a decisive knock-out victory might compel Washington to halt its aggression. The later strategy called for risk and boldness, something that the South's two greatest military leaders had plenty of – Lee and Jackson.

Robert E. Lee and his trusted subordinate Thomas J. Jackson were acutely attuned to the fact that wars were not won on the defense. Although the Army of Northern Virginia racked up several impressive defensive victories both believed that only an aggressive thrust into the territory of the Union would help dampen the Yankee appetite for continued bloodshed.

Unfortunately, Jefferson Davis did not fully appreciate their vision. Nowhere is this lack of understanding from Richmond better illustrated than in Lee's greatest gamble for victory in the summer of 1863. When Robert E. Lee launched a second invasion of the United States, his Army of Northern Virginia should have been given every available soldier to achieve a much-needed win which might have ended the War. General Lee spent three full days in Richmond lobbying for his plan and pressing Davis and his cabinet for more men and supplies. It mostly fell on deaf ears. Although they ultimately acquiesced to Lee's plan to go on the offensive, Davis shortsightedly held back the needed resources to help ensure success. Davis even ignored Lee's final plea for at least the return of some of his detached brigades, which were then stationed on guard duty in Richmond and North Carolina. As it turned out, five full brigades from Lee's own army, a total of 11,000 experienced infantrymen of the highest order, where withheld. Gettysburg was lost.

Not only should Davis have provided the 11,000 battle hardened veterans to Lee, he should have stripped other commands for an additional 50,000! With Washington threatened by Lee, Richmond and most of the Confederacy were completely safe from new Union military attacks. Grant's western divisions were busy at far off Vicksburg on the Mississippi.

Nevertheless, despite all the miscalculations, blunders, and "what ifs" it was not a foregone conclusion that the South would lose its bid for freedom. Americans had won against long odds in the past and the War could have gone the other way, particularly when one adds to the equation the fact that the Southern people were fighters and would not go down without one hell of a struggle.

Indeed, recognizing the herculean challenges facing the Confederacy in every category of necessity, it is a thing of amazement that they were ever able to even raise, arm, and equip a viable military force. Not only was the newborn nation limited in manpower but it stood entirely deficient in the "sinews of war, and in the means to produce them."[227] With no reserves of clothing, food, equipment, and lacking a proper organizational structure to undertake the huge task of supply and equipment, the central government was forced to rely upon the States. In a pattern reminiscent of the Revolutionary War, the States were asked to supply and equip their own men with the promise of future reimbursement by Richmond. Given the agrarian nature of the region and the total naivety of what an invasion by the United States might actually entail, the actual progress made in just the first two years borders on the incredible.

Southerners fully understood that only a vibrant military could defend and preserve the independence of the nation. Hard work by all and neighborly charity went hand-in-hand in the South,[228] yet the Confederacy had no military. Instead, mixed together within a strong paternalistic framework, it had hundreds of thousands of non-slave owning, independently minded, dirt/subsistence farmers; some skilled laborers; large numbers of enslaved Americans; almost a quarter million free blacks; and a handful of the landed gentry. Such was the material that would provide the logistical support and fill the ranks of the companies, regiments, and brigades. Around a small cadre of professional soldiers who had resigned from the "old Army," the Confederate States of America would have to move quickly to mold an effective military.

Because it was the State's responsibility to raise regiments for the Confederate Army, they were also expected to feed and clothe their own men sent to the field, while still providing for the limited governmental needs of their citizens on the home front. Hundreds of Confederate depots were set up in each State to collect supplies and most Southern governors understood the necessity to support the authorities in Richmond, but others like Governor Joseph Brown of Georgia made it very clear that their first priority was to their State troops and not to the Confederacy.[229]

Southerners could boast of Southern ingenuity and courage, but with very few manufacturing facilities, the primary sources for equipping the armies were by means of captured Federal materials, blockade runners bringing in arms from Europe, or smugglers from Mexico hauling supplies across the Rio Grande River into Texas. Arms and ammunition took top priority with clothing, including uniforms, shoes, and blankets, second. General consumer goods were luxury items.

Even with all the impossibilities, the nascent nation of the Confederate States of America was bubbling with excitement in the early months of independence. By February 1, 1861, seven States had withdrawn from the United States and set up a provisional capital in Montgomery, Alabama. The hardships of wartime had not yet come and everywhere there was a sense of purpose so that when war actually broke out, high pitched patriotic fever in the South overwhelmed the capability of the government to arm and equip the volunteers. So many thousands spontaneously rushed to join the military in early 1861, that the Confederacy had to turn away approximately 200,000 men. Again, conventional thinking at the time was that the War would be over by Christmas of 1861, and those that were accepted and organized into fighting units signed enlistment contracts for only one year of service per an act of Congress passed in March 1861.

At first things went well for the Confederacy and the South won a stunning victory at Manassas, Virginia, in July of 1861. With Lincoln at the helm, however, the Union Anaconda strategy soon kicked in to cripple the entire South, but it was always Richmond (the capital moved from Montgomery to Richmond when Virginia seceded in April 1861) just a mere 109 miles from Washington City, that was the plumb jewel. Nevertheless, to their great consternation, the Federals discovered that it was a "long road to Richmond" but the blue masses in and around Washington would regroup after each defeat by Lee's Army of Northern Virginia and return again and again.

With the Union army boosted to 660,000 strong by December 1861, the Confederacy responded with the Enrollment Act of April 16, 1862, which provided mandatory enlistment in the military for three years or the duration of the War for all able-bodied white males of military age, unless exempted. While the Confederate Congress amended the conscription laws several times over the course of the War to recruit wider and wider categories, everyone knew that all must do their duty if there was to be any chance to repel the invading armies.

Some of the categories of exemption included Confederate or State officials, railroad workers, mail carriers, ferrymen on post-office routes, river pilots, telegraph operators, miners, printers, certain teachers, workers in cotton and wool factories, preachers, doctors, factory owners, shoemakers, millers, tanners, blacksmiths, wagon makers, and even those morally opposed to war (provided they furnished a substitute and paid $500). Interestingly, on every working plantation with twenty or more enslaved people, or 500 head of cattle, or 250 head of horses, one white man was entitled to an exemption. This exemption was not a free pass to the wealthy as some falsely alleged, but was designed to ensure that the agricultural base would continue to supply necessary foodstuffs to the Confederacy – the big producing farmer could better serve the South by farming corn than by fighting. The slanderous slogan of "a rich man's war and a poor man's fight"[230] was largely a fictional charge. Actually, as it turned out, most of the sons of planters and the planters themselves disregarded the exemption and joined the military anyway. Ultimately, unless granted an exemption, all white males between 17 and 50 years of age where required to serve, if not in the Confederate armed forces, then at least in the State Guard (these troops did not have to serve beyond the borders of their State).[231]

The first Conscription Act caused an immediate response from the loyal population that was now liable for service and across the South men rushed to volunteer before being drafted, which was deemed by most communities as a disgrace and an affront to male honor. In any event, with the new law there was now no discretion about the need to stay at home to care for the family vs. the need to serve the Confederacy. Unfortunately, by early 1864, the military could expect no more white males to enlist – they were all gone. In April 1864, he Confederate Secretary of War informed President Davis:

> [F]resh material for the armies can no longer be estimated as an element of future calculation for their increase, and necessity demands the invention of devices for keeping in the ranks the men now borne on the rolls .... For conscription from the general population, the functions of this Bureau [Bureau of Conscription] may cease with the termination of the year 1864.[232]

All told, approximately 750,000 men served in the Confederate military (compared with 2,865,000 in the North) with an astonishing 75-85 percent of the military-age white males in the South eventually donning uniforms.[233] Of that number well over half were either dead or wounded by the time the War ended! About 258,000 died by disease or from wounds received on the battlefield and another 200,000 were wounded.[234] In Alabama alone, 30,000 of her sons gave their lives fighting for the Confederacy.

The number of black Southerners, both free and enslaved, that died of disease or were killed or wounded in the struggle is unknown but certainly tens of thousands served in various supply and support roles in the military, with a handful in actual combat roles. After two years into the War, Lincoln wisely employed and armed black soldiers to fight, while Davis and the Confederate Congress were far too late in this regard. Ignoring earlier pleas in 1864, by Lee and other high ranking Southern generals to grant freedom to all black Southerners that enlisted in the Rebel armies, the Confederate Congress ultimately passed such a law on March 13, 1865, the Act was entitled: "*An Act to Increase the Military Force of the Confederate States.*"[235] Under the new law each State was to furnish a quota of "volunteering" slaves, arming and enrolling a total of 300,000 men in combat roles who would then secure their freedom after honorable service to the nation.[236]

One can only wonder about the impact on both the War and the post-War era if the Confederacy had enacted this law in 1862, instead of 1865. General Lee told Englishman Herbert Saunders in 1866:

> [T]here was scarcely a Virginian now who was not glad that the subject [emancipation of slaves] had been definitely settled, though nearly all regretted that they had not been wise enough to do it themselves in the first year of the war.[237]

In *Confederate War*, a groundbreaking study on Southern morale and support for their nation, author Gary Gallagher shows through letters, diaries, and newspapers that the Southern people were strongly committed by a "tenacious popular will rooted in a sense of national community" that was unshaken by Union terror policies.[238] "Persevering despite great adversity, they surrendered only when their pool of manpower had been ravaged,"[239] not because of Union terror tactics on their people.

Paradoxically, only the military defeat of Robert E. Lee would signal the demise of the Confederate States of America.[240] Only that event would convince the people of the South that it was over. Thus, if Sherman truly desired to end the War expeditiously, as he claimed, he could have done more to affect that outcome by moving his armies immediately into Virginia when Atlanta fell in September 1864, to attack Lee's soldiers from the rear (Grant was then to Lee's front) and not bring terror on innocent, helpless civilians.

Chapter Seven

WAR CRIMES SOUTH

"As I have said before, if the guilty parties [Union forces pillaging civilians] could be taken, either the officer who commands, or the soldier who executes such atrocities, I should not hesitate to advise the infliction of the extreme punishment they deserve, but I cannot think it right or politic, to make the innocent ... suffer for the guilty."[241]

– Robert E. Lee

THERE IS NO QUESTION that the Confederacy also engaged in violations of the law of war, but comparing Southern violations to the violations of the Union is like comparing a mountain to a mole hill. While it is true that in the final months before the end of the War that some Confederate cavalry regiments in the Western Theater of operations confiscated fodder and food from local farmers to nourish themselves and their starving mounts without providing compensation, they did so only because the government had become incapable of providing provisions and they were forced to sustain themselves in the field. The gray horsemen were fighting a last-ditch effort on the home front, for the home front, and Richmond had authorized this emergency measure.

In turn, the occasional actual war crimes against person or property that were committed were not command directed in nature but rather performed by individuals in their individual capacity. In other words, the violations were not by design or direction from superiors as was the case with the Union's open policy of employing terrorism. Ironically, the greatest war crimes laid at the feet of the Confederacy – the acts of William Quantrill and his band of ruffians in the border States – is grossly misplaced. Quantrill was never commissioned as a Confederate officer and Richmond absolutely disavowed any connection with him and his renegade band of bushwhackers.[242]

So, given the appalling record of Union war crimes against Southern civilians, the more pertinent question which the reasonable observer cannot help but ask is why didn't the Confederacy vigorously engage in targeted acts of reprisal against Northern civilians as clearly provided for by Articles 27-28 of the Lieber Code? In a nutshell, the answer to this conundrum is largely associated with the person and character of Robert E. Lee.

First, since almost all of the actual combat actions took place on Southern soil the Confederacy had little opportunity to target Northern civilians for reprisals, expect on two major occasions when Robert E. Lee's Army of Northern Virginia ventured North into Maryland in 1862, and then Pennsylvania in 1863. In fact, the only Union town in the entire War that was destroyed by Confederate forces was Chambersburg, Pennsylvania, in the late summer of 1864. In response to the horrendous massive burnings of farms and homes in the Shenandoah Valley that summer by Major General "Black Dave" Hunter, [243] Confederate General Jubal Early ordered a cavalry strike across the Potomac River in order to conduct a targeted act of reprisal under the strict provisions of the Lieber Code. Unfortunately, the Union was not dissuaded from committing future war crimes in the Shenandoah Valley, which they literally burned to the ground. Again, the sole purpose of a lawful reprisal is to convince the enemy to stop their violations of the law of war. Early did this correctly, but without authorization from General Lee or Richmond.

Second, and most importantly, the South had the impeccable Robert E. Lee to both inspire and lead them. In truth, Lee did more to set the tone for ethical conduct on and off the battlefield than all the laws and codes put together could ever do.

General Robert E. Lee, 1862.

By any measure of judgment, the Army of Northern Virginia was the greatest army ever formed on American soil. But great armies are neither created nor sustained by accident. To a large degree, great armies are energized by officers who understand and then are able to apply the lessons of military history. In this respect, no officer truly can be called a professional without a firm commitment to the moral and ethical rules regulating combat activities. Quite naturally, this objective requires an ethos which consists of constant training for the troops and firm leadership from the commander, as well as a comprehensive understanding of one's moral roots. For Lee and many in the South, these core principles of morality and humanity were drawn from the Holy Bible.

Men of all classes and character can be found in the military, some possessed with good principles, showing that they have been well raised, but some so low on the scale of moral degradation that they have no self-respect, and of course, zero respect or empathy for anyone else. Knowing that the ugly realties attendant to warfare place great stresses on all soldiers, there invariably arises untoward temptations to engage in wrongdoing – from petty acts of moral turpitude to actual war crimes. Coupled with the Biblical truth that human nature is morally flawed and corrupt from birth *ab initio*, strong military discipline is an essential ingredient. Primarily, this command-and-control obligation to keep the troops in line is the responsibility of the commander. At all command positions, leadership is absolutely tasked with controlling the rank and file to ensure compliance with the humanitarian provisions of the law of war.

Thus, while the ingredients of victory are a combination of many factors – from logistics to training to armament – history has shown that one of the most important elements in a successful combat operation is the quality of the commander and his ability to control his men on and off the field of battle. The commander decides the strategy, directs the tactics, and inspires the morale of his soldiers. He is their role model. Such was Lee.

Conclusion

DISPELLING THE MYTHS

"Our men will fight you as long as they live and these boys [the children by her side] will fight you when they grow up."[244]
— *Southern Woman*

THE GROSS NATURE OF SHERMAN'S violations of the Lieber Code constitute war crimes of the highest order and cannot be excused by distorting the law of war or *reimagining* the facts. As stated, Sherman was not alone in this Union policy, he was only the most notorious executor of the policy. Most certainly, even without the black letter law set out in the Lieber Code the enormity of the Union's use of terror on civilians was so spiteful and cruel that it will forever shock the conscience of humanity. It was pure madness.

Perhaps the real point of tragedy that must forever accompany the Union's use of terror is that neither General Sherman nor any of Lincoln's generals were ever held accountable for the barbarous outrages committed against innocent noncombatants. There were never any Congressional hearings or investigations, only a huge victory parade for Sherman and the others on May 23-24, 1865, in Washington City.

As demonstrated throughout this book, if Sherman were theoretically to stand trial for his violations of the law of war at a war crimes tribunal, his own words would provide damning testimony against him. There is no paucity of evidence to convict him and the justifications which might be raised offer no lawful defense whatsoever. The irrefutable facts of his command approved acts of terror would certainly result in a conviction by a jury of his peers for a wide array of grave breaches of the Lieber Code.

In today's setting, if any American general followed Sherman's example of "total war" on civilians he would not only be guilty of numerous war crimes, but the army he commanded and the nation he represented would be rightly subjected to the scorn and ridicule of the entire civilized world.[245] Even by the somewhat less rigid standards of his own day, General Sherman left nothing worth emulating.

– The Myth of Sherman the Great –

General Sherman began work on this memoirs just after 1870, and in 1875, *Memoirs of General W. T. Sherman* was published as a two volume set and so sprang forth the myth of "Sherman the great," a view that is fully embraced by the vast majority of modern Sherman commentators.[246] Ignoring his bright line violations of the law of civilized warfare, these modern-day purveyors of "fake history" might grudgingly admit that Sherman's actions against civilians were controversial, but they inevitably spew out base nonsense that one simply can't pass "moral judgments"[247] on the matter. Others simply go on the offensive and attack anyone who dares criticize Sherman's use of terrorism as deluded advocates for the "Lost Cause."[248] This fictitious version of Sherman is so powerful that to pose any opposition is to be un-American or even ... a "domestic extremist." Indeed, the myth is so strong that the truth seems to no longer matter. For example, a typical handling of the topic is found in the preface of a study of Sherman's movement across Georgia where the so-called historian absolutely refuses to condemn the Union war crimes and terrorism.

> My objective, however, is *neither to condemn nor condone the behavior of Sherman and his men. As I see it, my job is not to cast moral judgments*

upon the conduct of others; rather, it is to ascertain exactly what they did and understand why they did it [emphasis added].[249]

Really? How it possible to not pass *moral judgments* on those responsible for intentionally causing profound suffering on unprotected women and children during winter? With homes burned down and all belongings taken or destroyed the effects of the atrocities would be felt the rest of their lives. How too, can one not pass a moral judgment on a senior military commander in the United States Army who intentionally poured out pure horror on noncombatants and boasted of it at every turn? Sherman's own words:

> There is a class of people men, women, and children, who must be killed or banished before you can hope for peace and order.[250]

If premeditated, cold-blooded, and deliberate cruelty does not demand condemnation from the civilized world, then what does? The true conclusion is that employing terror tactics against large groups of civilians makes Lincoln's Union guilty of disregarding the Lieber Code, the canons of West Point, the laws of nations, and the customary rules of civilized warfare as they then existed. Not only are the enormities too well documented to sweep under the collective rug of ignorance, but the guilt must forever rest upon the heads of those who terrorized the innocent and helpless women and children of the South. For the first time in American history, a "vast region had been scorched and despoiled and war taken to women, children, and the aged."[251] One historian describes the true legacy of the terrorist W. T. Sherman as follows:

> Sherman must rank as the first of the modern totalitarian generals. He made war universal, *waged it on the enemy's people* and not only on armed men, and *made terror the linchpin of his strategy*. To him more than any other man must be attributed the hatred that grew out of the Civil War [emphasis added].[252]

The Union's barbaric acts deserve condemnation, not accolades. Clear thinkers must never conflate the positive of ending slavery with any of the so-called justifications for terrorism on civilians.

– LEE –

In no form or fashion was Sherman qualified to command. Nor was he what some historians would call a "modern soldier," effectively pursuing the new realities of modern warfare and unshackling himself from the old methods. Clearly, the modern soldier definition applies to the application of lawful combat tactics that keep pace with the technology, not the abandonment of ethics in how violence is applied on or off the battlefield. If that label applies to anyone during the War it belonged to Lee and his most effective subordinate, Stonewall Jackson. In addition, his soldiers were *followers* of General Lee, "with a sense of discipleship that was given to no other commanding general in the war."[253] According to one military writer:

> Lee and Jackson did not see themselves as old soldiers; they considered themselves modern soldiers, and today's officers will quickly learn to identify with them.[254]

Apart from being the most enduring conflict in the nation's psyche, the War brought into focus the extraordinary genius and person of General R. E. Lee – a commander and role model so phenomenal that his impact upon the armed forces of the United States is still felt over a hundred and fifty years after his death. This is not surprising when one considers that even before the outbreak of the War, Lee's military value was already firmly recognized in the young nation.

General Winfield Scott, commander of the American forces during the Mexican War (1846-1848), noted on many occasions that the war was won due largely to the efforts of then, Captain Robert E. Lee. Captain Lee had made such an impression on Scott that thirteen years later, in 1861, when asked by the Lincoln Administration who was the best officer in the United States military, he promptly replied:

> I tell you, sir, that Robert E. Lee is the greatest soldier
> now living, and if he ever gets the opportunity, he will
> prove himself the greatest captain of history.[255]

President Abraham Lincoln was also well acquainted with Lee's military acumen. In April 1861, before Colonel Lee, then serving in the 2nd United States Cavalry, had to decide between loyalty to Virginia or the Union, Lincoln eagerly tendered to Lee the supreme command of all Union forces in the field. If he had accepted, Lee would have been second only to General Scott, the aging and soon to retire general-in-chief of the United States military. Weighing a devoted career spanning over thirty years of service to the armed forces of the United States against his attachment to the inherent rights of Virginia and her people, Lee turned down this greatest of all opportunities.[256] Taken to the mountain top of temptation and offered what many a soldier dreams of – fantastic success and fame – Lee maintained his loyalty to his State and family, thereby reflecting to the world a glimpse of his incredible integrity and honor. As with George Washington, honor and duty were more important than fame and fortune. Lee could not draw his sword against his native State, nor tolerate unconstitutional violence by the Lincoln Administration to force a so-called "government of the consent" on his fellow Americans now populating those States that no longer consented to be so governed.[257] Lee wrote to his daughter in January 1861:

> If the bond of the Union can only be maintained by the
> sword and the bayonet, instead of brotherly love and
> friendship, [the Union] will lose all interest with me
> ... I can, however, do nothing but trust to the wisdom
> and patriotism of the nation and to the overruling
> providence of a merciful God.[258]

Despite the ignorance and blindness inherent in the "cancel culture" which now infects much of modern America and seeks to obliterate all public recognition of America's great heroes of the past, to objective and rational Americans Lee's name has only increased in brightness, illuminating the pages of military doctrine and professionalism as perhaps no other soldier in American history.[259]

Lee is the personification of the spirit of Americanism and of true Southern manhood, contributing more than any other single officer in setting the very bedrock for some of the most outstanding and valuable attributes of American military power. That bedrock is so strong today that when asked to identify the most notable characteristics of the United States military, one should expect the worldwide response to literally echo Lee's signature, even if political correctness keeps his name from their lips – superior tactical and strategic abilities in combat leaders and the highest level of civilized conduct in warfare.[260]

The antithesis of Sherman, General Robert E. Lee was not only recognized as a military genius, but he was also praised equally by North and South for his morality and careful adherence to the law of war, particularly in the protection of the property and persons of innocent civilians. In contrast to Lincoln's total war policy against Southern civilians, Lee insisted upon a strict interpretation of the rule of law when it came to the treatment of Northern civilians. There were no slick, duplicitous "forage liberally" orders issued by Lee to target helpless Union women and children. Lee never subjected Northerners to the terror and horror that was visited upon his own people and to those who have even casually studied the man objectively, they understand that Lee knew no other way.

In April 1861, when General Scott received Lee's resignation from the United States Army in order to offer his services to the Confederacy, Scott expressed the greatest regret. What consoled the old general, however, was knowing that Lee would strictly abide by the law of war if fighting broke out, particularly when it came to protecting innocent civilians. Scott prophetically remarked:

> [The United States] would have as his opponent a soldier worthy of every man's esteem, and one who would conduct the war upon the strictest rules of civilized warfare. There would be no outrages committed upon the private persons or property which he could prevent.[261]

On both of his military campaigns into the North, Sharpsburg in 1862, and Gettysburg in 1863, Lee conducted his army impeccably, severely punishing those soldiers who were caught engaging in larceny or destruction of private property.[262] There was no marauding, no looting, no burning, and no brutalizing of civilians. Even though many of his poor soldiers had not worn shoes for almost a year and were in desperate need of proper clothing and good food, General Lee stickily forbade his men from entering any private homes in search of supplies and all foods or goods requisitioned from private store owners were paid for in Confederate money or script, to be redeemed later. In turn, straggling behind the main columns of march, which might provide opportunities for malcontents to fall out and pillage, was also strictly forbidden and enforced to the letter by strong provost guards following the march. Union town after town fell without a shot being fired or a home desecrated. No destruction of private property was permitted under any circumstances.

Although fully knowledgeable about Union terror acts that had intentionally razed civilian homes and farms in many areas of the South, Lee personally issued two general orders to keep close rein on his ill-clothed and hungry soldiers as they marched across Northern farmlands in 1863. In accordance with the true meaning of "military necessity" under the Lieber Code – when the army is in need of provisions to sustain itself in enemy territory – General Order No. 72, was issued on June 21, 1863:

> [C]hiefs of the commissary, quartermaster, ordinance and medical departments of the army" [to make] requisitions upon the local authorities or inhabitants for the necessary supplies [to sustain the army] shall be paid the market price for the articles furnished.[263]

Of course there were isolated instances where some individuals in Lee's army and cavalry did commit crimes against Northern civilians, primarily stealing horses and clothing, but these instances were few in number, almost always punished, and certainly the exception, not the rule.[264] Without question, the primary reason that the disciplined behavior of the Southern solider stood in such startling contrast to the revolting behavior of his Northern counterpart was due to the leadership factor and stern discipline. Lee's command and control actions comported perfectly with the Lieber Code and its allowance for military necessity, while Sherman's conduct was a complete exercise in hypocrisy and deceit.

In fact, Lee was greatly pleased with the conduct of his army as it made its way into Pennsylvania in June of 1863, and issued General Order No. 73 on June 27, 1863, both to remind them of their obligations under the law of war as soldiers and as Christians.

Head-Quarters Army of Northern Virginia,

Chambersburg, Pa., June 27th 1863

General Order No. 73

The commanding general has observed with marked satisfaction the conduct of the troops on the march, and confidently anticipates results commensurate with the high spirit they have manifested....

Their conduct in other respects has, with few exceptions, been in keeping with their character as soldiers, and entitles them to approbation and praise.

There have, however, been instances of forgetfulness on the part of some that they have in keeping the yet unsullied reputation of this army, and that the duties exacted of us by civilization and Christianity are not less obligatory in the country of the enemy than in our own.

The commanding general considers that no greater disgrace can befall the army, and through it, our whole people, than the perpetration of barbarous outrages upon the unarmed and defenseless, and the wanton destruction of private property, that have marked the course of the enemy in our own country. Such proceedings not only degrade the perpetrators and all connected with them, but are subversive of the discipline and efficiency of the army, and destructive of the ends of our present movement.

It must be remembered that we make war only upon armed men, and that we cannot take vengeance for the wrongs our people have suffered without lowering ourselves in the eyes of all whose abhorrence has been excited by the atrocities of our enemies [Union terrorism], and offending to whom vengeance belongeth, without whose favor and support our efforts must all prove in vain.

The commanding general, therefore, earnestly exhorts the troops to abstain, with most scrupulous care, from unnecessary or wanton injury to private property, and he enjoins upon all officers to arrest and bring to summary punishment all who shall in any way offend against orders on this subject.[265]

R. E. LEE, General

Although some members of the government criticized Lee for not authorizing lawful reprisals to force the enemy to cease what many could see was an evolving pattern of disregard for the Lieber Code, particularly in the Western Theater where Union cavalry raids were increasingly engaged in burning down towns and villages in Tennessee, northern Mississippi, and northern Alabama, General Lee firmly believed that reprisals were not the answer. Responding to an 1864 letter from the Confederate Secretary of War regarding possible Confederate retaliation to what by then had become clear to all – a conscious Union policy of visiting massive terror on civilians – Lee reiterated his position in the summer of 1864:

As I have said before, if the guilty parties could be taken, either the officer who commands, or the soldier who executes such atrocities, I should not hesitate to advise the infliction of the extreme punishment they deserve, but I cannot think it right or politic, to make the innocent ... suffer for the guilty.[266]

Apart from the influence of Christian ethics on his thinking and action, with Americans fighting Americans Lee knew that the long-term effects of engaging in retribution or reprisal would not be profitable for the nation or the South. He was undoubtedly correct; Lee's strict adherence to the rules regulating warfare, coupled with his firm policy prohibiting reprisals, contributed greatly to the healing process after the War, particularly in the Northern States. At the end of the day, one of the driving forces that created the legend of Lee, the ultimate gentleman, was his unmatched sense of humanity. One biographer observed that "Lee was the soldier-gentleman of tradition, generous, forgiving, silent in the face of failure ... a hero of mythology."[267] Thus, no matter how great the temptation for revenge, R. E. Lee would not stoop to the level of his enemies. This is one of the reasons he was labeled the "Christian General," by both North and South.[268]

The ethical conduct of Lee as well as the overwhelming majority of Southern commanders across the spectrum of command is evident and historically verifiable, as is the torrid conduct of Sherman and his ilk. The difference, of course, was that Lee, in lawful combat, directed his ferocity toward legitimate military targets of the enemy, while Sherman often directed his ferocity at unarmed and helpless civilians. Similarly, when the end came for Lee and the Confederacy at Appomattox Court House on April 9, 1865, his decision to surrender the Army of Northern Virginia rather than to disband it was perhaps one of Lee's greatest moments. Lee could have ordered his decimated soldiers to scatter into the hills and fight a guerrilla war that would have lasted for decades. Instead, he saw no sense in waging a war of terror and ordered his men to lay down their arms, return home, and become once again model citizens. And so, when word of Lee's unequivocal surrender was learned, the rest of the Confederacy quickly followed suit and reflexively laid down their arms as well – Lee was their moral and military leader, not Jefferson Davis. It is not an inaccurate assessment that the Confederacy lasted as long as it did because of him and when he quit, the nation ceased to be.

To the objective mind, Sherman's legacy is one of shame, while Lee's is one of glory. Perhaps the most telling tribute to Lee came from his former enemies. When General Lee passed into his eternity in 1870, just five years after the War, newspapers throughout the North universally praised both his military genius and high standard of morality.[269] The *New York Herald* said:

> In him the military genius of America was developed to a greater extent than ever before. In him all that was pure and lofty in mind and purpose found lodgment. He came nearer the ideal of a soldier and Christian general than any man we can think of.[270]

In a speech given in 1874, Senator Benjamin H. Hill of Georgia summed up the true greatness of General Robert Edward Lee as follows:

> He was a foe without hate, a friend without treachery, a soldier without cruelty, a victor without oppression, and a victim without murmuring. He was a public officer without vices, a private citizen without wrong, a neighbor without reproach, a Christian without hypocrisy, and a man without guile. He was Caesar without his ambition, Frederick without his tyranny, Napoleon without his selfishness and Washington without his reward.[271]

In closing, the Civil War is unique in large part because one cannot yet speak of it as something from the past. On the other hand, there really are no "symbols of a bygone era" because in part, many Southerners stubbornly embrace the root principles that caused America's Founding Fathers to pick up their weapons – defense of their homes and a firm belief in limited government. Neither fear, suffering, nor terror will deter a people who belong to "the home of the brave and the land of the free."[272] Such stalwarts as these are the salt of the nation.

Endnotes

1   Rebecca West (Cicely Isabel Fairfield), *The Meaning of Treason* (1949), 311.

2   *See* J. David Hacker, "A Census-Based Count of the Civil War Dead," *Civil War History* (2011), Issue 4, 307, 311. Demographic historian J. David Hacker's groundbreaking research based on 19th century census data disclosed that the previous accepted estimates of 600,000 soldier deaths was far too low.

3   Douglas Southall Freeman, *R. E. Lee: A Biography* (1934), Vol. IV, 401.

4   *See* Ross K. Baker, "Voices: Democrats Foolishly Purge Heroes," *USA Today*, Aug. 11, 2015, A2.

5   *See, e.g.,* Thomas Buell, *The Warrior Generals* (1997) [hereinafter *The Warrior Generals*].

6   Jeffrey F. Addicott, *Radical Islam Why?* (2016), 1.

7   *See* Michael Andrew Grissom, *American Terrorists, Lincoln's Armies in the South* (2015).

8   *See* Caleb Carr, *The Lessons of Terror: A History of Warfare Against Civilians* (2002), 17–30. This work discusses how terrorism is a tactic associated with violence in war and peace.

9   Estanislao Oziewicz, *Annan Proposes Definition of Terrorism*, Center for International Governance Innovation (March 21, 2005), www.bit.ly/3QmBdF5 (last visited Jan. 05, 2023).

10   Jeffrey F. Addicott, *The Abu Ghraib Story*, 2; Israeli Defense Forces L. Rev. (2006), 35, 37.

11   *See* James M. McPherson, *Crossroads of Freedom: Antietam (Pivotal Moments in American History) (2002)*, 15, 70. In a letter to a Democratic friend, General McClellan told him he was "fighting to preserve the integrity of the Union." *Ibid.*

12   Richard B. Harwell, *The Confederate Reader: How the South Saw the War* (1989), 219.

13   David Smith, *Sherman's March to the Sea 1864: Atlanta to Savannah* (2007), 90. [hereinafter *Sherman's March*].

14   LTC Ryan Dowdy, JA, USA, Chair et al., *Law of Armed Conflict Deskbook* (5th ed. 2015), 10, 13.

15   *See* Jeffrey F. Addicott, *Terrorism Law: Materials, Cases, Comments* (7th ed. 2014), 274-275.

16   *See generally* Walter Brian Cisco, *War Crimes Against Southern Civilians* (2007) [hereinafter *War Crimes Against Southern Civilians*].

17   Some writers believe that this phrase was taken from a speech made by Sherman in 1880. Sherman said, "There is many a boy here today who looks on war as all glory, but, boys, it is all hell." From this sentence the newspapers coined the phrase, "War is hell." Other sources attribute the phrase to an 1879 address made before the Michigan Military Academy where Sherman remarked, "I am tired and sick of war. Its glory is all moonshine ... War is hell." *Ibid. See* Justin Wintle, The Dictionary of War Quotations (1989), 91.

18   *See* Michael Andrew Grissom, *American Terrorists: Lincolns Armies in the South* (2015).

19   *See* Richard Shelly Hartigan, *Lieber's Code and the Law of War* (1983), 18. [hereinafter *Lieber Code*] (Citations to War Department General Order 100 are referenced to the specific article contained within the Order).

20   U.S. War Department, *War of the Rebellion: A Compilation of the Official Records of the Union and Confederate Armies* (Washington D.C. 1880-1901) Ser. 2, Vol. 5, 149-164. [hereinafter OR]; *Civil War Records: Basic Research Sources*, National Archives (Sept. 4, 2018), www.bit.ly/3Z7fB3w (Last visited Jan. 05, 2023). General Order 100 contains specific paragraphs set out in the *Official Records of the War of the Rebellion. See also* Dietrich Schindler & Jiri Toman, *The Laws of Armed Conflict* (1988), 3.

21   *See generally* Gary D. Solis, "The Law of Armed Conflict: International Humanitarian Law," *War* (2010), 3–7. Provides a good thumbnail history of the origin and development of the law of war.

22   *Field Manual*, 6-27, *The Commander's Handbook on the Law of Land Warfare,* (Aug. 7, 2019) [hereinafter FM 6-27], 1-7, at 1-2. The Manual provides a general description of the law of land warfare, but notes the *Department of Defense Law of War Manual* (Dec. 2016) is the authoritative statement on the law of war for the Department of Defense.

23   Customary international law consists of all those binding norms recognized and practiced by nations. *See* Restatement (Third) of the Foreign Relations Law of the United States § 102 (Am. Law Inst. 1986). Outlining principles of customary international law and providing comments as to how nations adhere to them.

24   The primary international treaty dealing with the law of war is the 1949 Geneva Conventions. The Geneva Conventions are set out in four categories: (1) Geneva Convention for the Amelioration of the Condition of the Wounded and Sick in Armed Forces in the Field, Aug. 12, 1949, for the Amelioration of the Condition of the Wounded and Sick in Armed Forces in the Field, 6 U.S.T. 3114, 75 U.N.T.S. 31; (2) Geneva Convention for the Amelioration of the Condition of Wounded, Sick and Shipwrecked Members of Armed Forces at Sea, Aug. 12, 1949, 6 U.S.T. 3217, 75 U.N.T.S. 85; (3) Geneva Convention Relative to the Treatment of Prisoners of War, Aug. 12, 1949, 6 U.S.T. 3316, 75 U.N.T.S. 135; and (4) Geneva Convention Relative to the Protection of Civilian Persons in Time of War, Aug. 12, 1949, 6 U.S.T. 3516, 75 U.N.T.S. 287. The primary international treaty dealing with the law of war is the 1949 Geneva Conventions. The Geneva Conventions are set out in four categories: (1) Geneva Convention for the Amelioration of the Condition of the Wounded and Sick in Armed Forces in the Field, Aug. 12, 1949, for the Amelioration of the Condition of the Wounded and Sick in Armed

Forces in the Field, 6 U.S.T. 3114, 75 U.N.T.S. 31; (2) Geneva Convention for the Amelioration of the Condition of Wounded, Sick and Shipwrecked Members of Armed Forces at Sea, Aug. 12, 1949, 6 U.S.T. 3217, 75 U.N.T.S. 85; (3) Geneva Convention Relative to the Treatment of Prisoners of War, Aug. 12, 1949, 6 U.S.T. 3316, 75 U.N.T.S. 135; and (4) Geneva Convention Relative to the Protection of Civilian Persons in Time of War, Aug. 12, 1949, 6 U.S.T. 3516, 75 U.N.T.S., 287.

25   *See* Lieber Institute, West Point, *About the Lieber Institute*, www.bit.ly/3GhjzOB (Last visited Jan. 05, 2023). West Point adopted the instruction on the *Lieber Code* in 1863, shortly after the code was promulgated.

26   *See* Frank Freidel, *Francis Lieber Nineteenth-Century Liberal* (1947), 8.

27   *Lieber Code*, Articles 45–71.

28   *Ibid.*, Article 15.

29   *See* Henry Putney Beers, *The Confederacy: A Guide to the Archives of the Government of the Confederate States of America* (2004), 142. The Confederate Articles of War was adopted by the Confederate Congress on March 6, 1861.

30   *Ibid.*, 142.

31   Department of Defense Directive 5100.77, 5.3.1, DoD Law of War Program (Dec. 9, 1998).

32   *Lieber Code*, at Article 18.

33   Like the Founders, Southerners viewed secession as a right derived from God. In this light, the post-War 1869 Supreme Court case of *Texas v. White* (5-3) which held that a State could not leave the Union is irrelevant. Secession is a God given right firmly set out in the Declaration of Independence and cannot be curtailed by any judicial ruling. *See Texas v. White* (1869), 74 U.S. (7 Wall.), 700.

34   Abraham Lincoln Papers: Series 1. General Correspondence. 1833-1916: Abraham Lincoln to Congress, January 12, 1848 (Speech Regarding the Mexican War) Library of Congress, Washington, D.C. 20540 USA, available at: www.bit.ly/3XcXqI7 (Last visited Jan. 05, 2023).

35   *Lieber Code*, Article 25.

36   *Ibid.*, Article 14.

37   *Ibid.*, Article 21.

38   *Ibid.*, Article 22.

39   *Ibid.*, Article 15.

40   *Ibid.*, Article 38.

41   *Ibid.*, Article 47.

42 *Ibid.*, Article 37.

43 *Ibid.*, Article 44.

44 *Ibid.*, Article 34.

45 *See* FM 6-27, 8-74 at 8-13.

46 Frank Freidel, *Francis Lieber Nineteenth-Century Liberal* (1947), 336.

47 *Lieber Code*, at Article 27.

48 Bruce Catton, *The Centennial History of the Civil War*, Vol. 1 The Coming Fury (1961), 424 [hereinafter *The Centennial History of the Civil War*]. Lincoln's consent to the terror policy.

49 Abraham Lincoln, Proclamation 80—Calling Forth the Militia and Convening an Extra Session of Congress (April 15, 1861), available at www.bit.ly/3CthgqB (05 January 2023).

50 *Letter from President Abraham Lincoln to James C. Conkling* (August 23,1863), available at LOC.gov: www.bit.ly/3CviKAy (Last visited Jan. 06, 2023).

51 *See* Elihu Root, *Addresses on International Subjects* (1916), 91. Available online at www.bit.ly/3imcx33 (Last visited Jan. 07, 2023).

52 *See* David Herbert Donald, *Lincoln* (1995), 410. President Lincoln consulted with General Halleck regularly.

53 For an excellent discussion on the topic of Lincoln's approval of the war crimes *see* David M. Thomas, *Abraham Lincoln and the Lieber Code: The Terrorism of the Confederate South* (2016).

54 William O. Stoddard, *Dispatches From the White House: The Anonymous Civil War Journalism of Presidential Secretary William O. Stoddard,* Michael Burlingame (2002), 93.

55 "The Present Aspect of the War – Causes for Hope," *New York Times*, 16 March 1864, 4.

56 Marc Wortman, *The Bonfire – The Siege and Burning of Atlanta* (2009), 208-209.

57 *Ibid.*, 93.

58 *See* Samuel W. Mitcham, Jr., *The Greatest Lynching in American History: New York 1863* (2020).

59 Robert G. McLendon, Jr., *History of the 53rd Regiment Alabama Volunteer Cavalry and M.W. Hannon's Cavalry Brigade Army of Tennessee, C.S.A.* (2007), 161.

60 *See* Marsha Landreth, *William T. Sherman* (1990), 46.

61   *Sherman's Civil War: Selected Correspondence of William T. Sherman 1860-1865* Brooks D. Simpson & Jean V. Berlin, eds. (1999), 617. [hereinafter *Selected Correspondence of William T. Sherman*].

62   Abraham Lincoln to William T. Sherman, December 26, 1864, *House Divided: The Civil War Research Engine at Dickinson College*, available at www.bit.ly/3vM4yzf (Last visited Jan. 07, 2023).

63   *Selected Correspondence of William T. Sherman*, 776. Russel F. Weigley, *History of the United States Army* (1984), 252.

64   Grady McWhiney, *The Civil War* (2005), 85.

65   *Ibid.*, 85-86.

66   *See* Albert Castel, *William Clarke Quantrill: His Life and Times* (1999), 103. William Quantrill was denied a commission in the Confederate military due to his disregard for the law of war.

67   *See* T. Henry Williams, *History of American Wars* (1981), 300-302.

68   *See William T. Sherman.*

69   *Ibid.*, 62.

70   Edward J. Stackpole, *They Met at Gettysburg* (1956), 27. [hereinafter *They Met at Gettysburg*].

71   *See* James Ronald Kennedy & Walter Donald Kennedy, *The South Was Right!* (1994). When the deep South seceded from the Union, Virginia at first voted to stay in the Union, but reversed itself and joined the Confederate States of America when President Lincoln ordered each "loyal" State to provide a quota of its citizens to form an army which would invade the Confederacy and force it back into the United States. The same reasoning led the slave holding States of North Carolina, Tennessee, and Arkansas to reverse loyalty to the United States and cast their lot with the Confederacy. The remaining slave States of Maryland, Kentucky, Delaware, and Missouri either split loyalties or elected to stay in the Union.

72   Letter from General Sherman to his wife, July 31, 1863, as cited in Thomas J. DiLorenzo, *The Real Lincoln* (2003), 184. [hereinafter *The Real Lincoln*].

73   Letter from Ellen Sherman to William T. Sherman, August 30, 1862. *See* Charles Bracelen Flood, *Grant and Sherman: The Friendship That Won the Civil War* (2006), 135.

74   *See* Michael R. Bradley, *With Blood and Fire* (2003), xvi. [hereinafter *Blood and Fire*].

75   Bruce Catton, *The Centennial History of the Civil War, The Coming Fury* (1961), Vol. 1, 424. [hereinafter *The Centennial History of the Civil War*].

76   Jacqueline Glass Campbell, *When Sherman Marched North From the Sea: Resistance on the Confederate Home Front* (2003), 33. [hereinafter *Resistance on the Confederate Home Front*] .

77   Joseph T. Glatthaar, *The March to the Sea and Beyond* (1985), 121. [hereinafter *The Sea and Beyond*].

78   Jim Miles, *To The Sea* (2002), 67-68. [hereinafter *To The Sea*].

79   *See* Carl Sandburg, *Abraham Lincoln: The Prairie Years and the War Years* (2007), 318. *See also,* John Fleishmann, "Union Colonel Phil Sheridan's Valiant Horse," *Smithsonian Magazine* (Nov. 1996), available at www.bit.ly/3WLuiaZ.

80   Acts 16:30-31. [A]nd after he [the Roman jailer] brought them [Paul and Silas from the collapse jail] out, he said, "Sirs, what must I do to be saved?" And they said, "Believe in the Lord Jesus, and you will be saved, you and your household [should do the same act of believing in Christ as Savior]." *Ibid.*

81   *See Blood and Fire*, xvi.

82   *See The Burning: Shenandoah Valley in Flames*, National Park Serv. (Dec. 21, 2021), available at www.bit.ly/3Crhlen.

83   Joseph Goldstein, Burke Marshall, & Jack Schwartz, *The My Lai Massacre and Its Cover-Up: Beyond the Reach of Law?* (1976), 554.

84   *Selected Correspondence of Sherman*, 730.

85   *Ibid.*, 731.

86   OR, Ser. 1, Vol. 32, Pt. 2, p. 132.

87   OR, Ser. I, Vol. 32, Pt. 3, p. 246.

88   *See* John Keegan, *The American Civil War: A Military History* (2009), 259.

89   *See* William Tecumseh Sherman, *Memoirs of General W. T. Sherman* (1990), 659. [hereinafter *Memoirs of General W. T. Sherman*].

90   *See* Lee Kennett, Marching *Through Georgia: The Story of Soldiers and Civilians During Sherman's Campaign* (1995), 287. [hereinafter *The Story of Soldiers and Civilians During Sherman's Campaign*].

91   *See Sherman's March*, 33.

92   *Lieber Code*, Article 44.

93   *Ibid.*, Article 14.

94   *Ibid.*, Article 15.

95   *Ibid.*, Article 16.

96   *See, e.g.*, Burke Davis, *Sherman's March* (1988), 69. [hereinafter *Sherman's March*].

97   *To The Sea*, 42.

98   Henry Hitchcock, *Marching With Sherman: Passages from the Letters and Campaign Diaries of Henry Hitchcock, Major and Assistant Adjutant General of Volunteers, November 1864-May 1865* (1927), 77.

99   *See* Frederic de Mulinen, "The Law of War and the Armed Forces," *International Review of the Red Cross* (1978), 18, 20.

100   *Memoirs of General W. T. Sherman*, 659.

101   Anne J. Bailey, *War and Ruin: William T. Sherman and the Savannah Campaign*, The American Crisis Series Books on the Civil War Era (2003), No. 10, xii.

102   *Ibid.*, 27.

103   *The Sea and Beyond*, 133.

104   Paul C. Graham, ed., *When the Yankees Come: Former South Carolina Slaves Remember Sherman's Invasion* (2016), 33. [hereinafter *When the Yankees Come*].

105   *To The Sea*, 125.

106   *When the Yankees Come*, 41.

107   *To The Sea*, 119.

108   *When the Yankees Come*, 37-38.

109   *See* Edward A. Pollard, *Southern History of the War* (1864), Vol. II 450-451.

110   *The Sea and Beyond*, 130.

111   *See* Grady McWhiney, *The Civil War* (2005), 134. To the author's credit, however, she correctly points out that after the War, Sherman waged a ruthless war "against American Indians in the West." *Ibid.*

112   *See* James J. Feigenbaum, James Lee & Filippo Mezzanotti, *Capital Destruction and Economic Growth: The Effects of Sherman's March, 1850-1920*, available at www.bit.ly/3ZwbeiX.

113   Justin Wintle, *The Dictionary of War Quotations* (1989), 281.

114   James Reston, Jr., *Sherman's March and Vietnam* (1989), 57.

115   *Sherman's March*, 33.

116   *The Sea and Beyond*, 125.

117   *See To The Sea*, 68. General Hitchcock could not get permission from General Sherman to hold role calls.

118   *See The Story of Soldiers and Civilians During Sherman's Campaign*, 273.

119   *Resistance on the Confederate Home Front*, 54.

120   *See The Sea and Beyond*, 133.

121   For example, despite numerous eyewitness accounts by his own soldiers to the contrary, Sherman always denied the burning of Columbia, blaming it on the retreating Confederate cavalry. *See* Bernard Davidson, *Who Burned Columbia?—A Review of General Sherman's View of the Affair* (1977), S. Hist. Soc'y Papers 185-92.

122   *See* Henry Hitchcock, *Marching with Sherman: Passages from the Letters and Campaign Diaries of Henry Hitchcock, Major and Assistant Adjutant General of Volunteers, November 1864-May 1865* (1995), 134. [hereinafter *Passages from the Letters and Campaign Diaries of Henry Hitchcock*].

123   *Passages from the Letters and Campaign Diaries of Henry Hitchcock*, 77.

124   David Nevin, *The Civil War: Sherman's March* (1986), 70.

125   *Ibid.*

126   *Ibid.*

127   *Ibid.*, 53. *See* also, Noah Andre Trudeau, *Southern Storm* (2008). 64.

128   Rudolph C. Barnes, Jr., *Military Legitimacy: Might and Right in the New Millennium* (1996), 26.

129   *Selected Correspondence of Sherman*, 761.

130   *Ibid.*, 776.

131   Margie Riddle Bearss, *Sherman's Forgotten Campaign – The Meridian Expedition* (1987), 215. [hereinafter *Meridian Expedition*].

132   OR, Ser. I, Vol. 32, Pt. 2, p. 471.

133   *Meridian Expedition*, 220.

134   *Ibid.*, 227.

135   William T. Sherman, *Memoirs of General William T. Sherman* (2007), Michael Fellman, ed., 547.

136   *Sherman's March*, 37.

137   Dr. Daniel Trezevant, a respected physician in Columbia, South Carolina, listed several cases of rape of which he had personal knowledge. *See* Rod Gragg, *Illustrated Confederate Reader* 192-196 (1989). *See* also James Reston, Jr, *Sherman's March and Vietnam* (1989), 73-74. In the city of Milledgeville, Georgia, only one rape of a white female could be substantiated by a respected writer and physician, Dr. James Bonner.

138   *See* Crystal N. Feimster, *Southern Horrors: Women and the Politics of Rape and Lynching* (2011), 20.

139   *Resistance on the Confederate Home Front*, 46.

140 *Ibid.*, 4.

141 Lloyd Lewis, *Sherman: Fighting Prophet* (1993), 440.

142 David P. Conyngham, *Sherman's March Through the South* (1865), 277.

143 *War Crimes Against Southern Civilians*, 175.

144 Michael Andrew Grissom, *American Terrorists: Lincoln's Armies in the South* (2015), 21. *See also* R. I. Holcombe, *History of Marion County* (2000), 491.

145 *Ibid.*, 331. *See also*, Jim Downs, Sick From Freedom: African-American Illness and Suffering During War and Reconstruction (2012). Puts the estimate at one million black Southerners who lost their lives, mostly through disease and starvation during the War through Reconstruction.

146 *The Sea and Beyond*, 52-65.

147 *Ibid.*, 58.

148 *See, e.g., To The Sea*, 316.

149 William Gilmore Simms, *Sack and Destruction of the City of Columbia, S.C.* (1865), 251-253.

150 Anne King Gregorie, *History of Sumter County* (1954).

151 Lewis G. Regenstein, "Sherman's March: How the History Channel Cleanses History," *Southern Partisan* (2007), Vol. 26, No. 2, at 23.

152 Joseph Goldstein et al., *The My Lai Massacre and Its Cover-Up: Beyond the Reach of Law?* (1976), 555.

153 *The Warrior Generals*, 384-385.

154 *See, e.g.,* John F. Marszalek, *Sherman: A Soldier's Passion for Order* (2007). *The author actually argues that Sherman had a respect for the law and an uncanny grasp of what modern democracies needed to do in warfare.*

155 Thomas Robertson, "The War in Words," *Civil War Times Illustrated*, Oct. 1979, 20.

156 *Ibid.*, 120.

157 *Law and Responsibility in Warfare: The Vietnam Experience* (1975), Peter D. Trooboff, ed., 77. Victor's justice refers to the view that the victorious side can prosecute or fail to prosecute anyone it wishes without regard to normal processes of law.

158 *See, e.g.,* John Bennet Walters, "General William T. Sherman and Total War," *Journal of Southern History* (1948), Vol. 14.3, 447-480; E. S. Corwin, *Total War and the Constitution* (1947).

159 OR, Ser. 2, Vol. 5, pp. 149-164.

160   Stephen Davis, *What the Yankees Did to Us: Sherman's Bombardment and Wrecking of Atlanta* (2012), 101.

161   *Lieber Code*, Article 47.

162   *See e.g.,* Mollie M. Madden, *The Black Prince and the Grande Chevauchée of 1355* (2018).

163   *See* notes 102, 163 and accompanying text.

164   *Selected correspondence of Sherman*, 617.

165   "Sherman's Grand March: A Picturesque Report by Himself," *New York Times,* Aug. 13, 1865, 2. Available at www.nyti.ms/3Cwldup.

166   *See e.g.,* Noah Andre Trudeau, *Southern Storm* (2008), 27.

167   *See* Joseph Goldstein et al., *The My Lai Massacre and Its Cover-Up: Beyond the Reach of Law?* (1975), 554.

168   *Ibid.*

169   *Selected Correspondence of Sherman*, 600.

170   OR, Ser. 1, Vol. 32, Pt. 2, p. 132.

171   *Selected Correspondence of Sherman*, 707-709. The Sept. 12, 1864, letter was in response to the mayor and other officials following the capture of Atlanta and Sherman's treatment of civilians trapped in the city.

172   Justin Wintle, *The Dictionary of War Quotations* (1989), 24. *See generally,* Arther Ferrill, *The Fall of the Roman Empire* (1986).

173   *Deuteronomy* 20:10-20.

174   Karen Stokes, "Sherman's War on Civilians in South Carolina: Excerpts from South Carolina Civilians in Sherman's Path," *Confederate Veteran*, Jan./Feb.2015, 57.

175   Jeffrey F. Addicott & William A. Hudson, Jr., "The Twenty-Fifth Anniversary of My Lai: Time to Inculcate the Lessons," *Mil. L. Rev.* (1993), 139,153, 169.

176   *Ibid.*

177   Edward G. Longacre, *Worthy Opponents: William T. Sherman & Joseph E. Johnston* (2006), 292.

178   *Ibid.*, 293.

179   *See Selected Correspondence of Sherman*, 657; Nick Overby, "Supplying Hell: The Campaign for Atlanta," *Quartermaster Professional Bulletin*, Winter 1992, 4-7.

180   Henry W. Halleck, *International Law; or Rules Regulating the Intercourse of States in Peace and War* (1861), 46.

181 *See* Glen W. LaForce, "The Trial of Major Henry Wirz: A National Disgrace," *The Army Lawyer*, (June 1988), 3.

182 *See* Stanley Weintraub, *General Sherman's Christmas, Savannah 1864* (2009), 167-168. Lincoln apparently was willing to overlook Sherman's crimes because of his success at Atlanta and capture of Savannah. In a December 26, 1864, letter the President praised him.

183 Anne J. Bailey, *War and Ruin: William T. Sherman and the Savannah Campaign* (2003), The American Crisis Series Books on the Civil War Era, no. 10, 136.

184 *Selected Correspondence of Sherman*, 701.

185 Dino A. Brugioni, "The Meanest Bushwhacker," *Blue and Gray*, (June 1991), 32, 34. Union General Thomas Ewing issued the order in the fall of 1863. In essence, all individuals residing in an area that covered four western counties in Missouri were given 15 days to evacuate. The homes, farms, and fields of some 20,000 dwellings were burned, and many of their personal valuables were stolen.

186 *See* Thomas DiLorenzo, *The Real Lincoln,* 173.

187 Mark A. Knoll, "The Struggle for Lincoln's Soul," *Christianity Today* Vol. 42, No. 2, Feb. 8, 1998.

188 For an excellent discussion on this topic, *see* Walter Donald Kennedy, *Rekilling Lincoln* (2015) 143-164.

189 *See* Mark Grimsley, *The Hard Hand of War: Union Military Policy Toward Southern Civilians, 1861-1865* (1995).

190 *American Collector: Inside the Civil War* (2021), Annabel Vered, ed., 61.

191 James Reston, Jr., *Sherman's March and Vietnam* (1989), 70. General Howard related this to Sherman on November 23, 1864.

192 *Ibid.* General Howard issued this order on November 24, 1864.

193 *See, e.g., The Sea and Beyond*, 58.

194 Russell F. Weigley, *History of the United States Army* (1984), 301.

195 John M. Gibson, *Those 163 Days* (1961), 56.

196 *See* W. Todd Groce, *Rethinking Sherman's March,* New York Times, opinion page, Nov. 17, 2014. Despite the title suggesting that Sherman should be blamed for his war crimes and use of terror, the author excuses and even praises him, placing the blame on the eleven Southern States for forming their own nation.

197 Justin Wintle, *The Dictionary of War Quotations,* 280.

198 *See Abraham Lincoln Papers: Series 2. General Correspondence. 1858-1864*: Abraham Lincoln to Horace Greeley, Friday, August 22, 1862 (clipping from Aug. 23, 1862 *Daily National Intelligencer*, Washington, D.C.).

199   *See* Robin Young, *For Love and Liberty: The Untold Civil War Story of Major Sullivan Ballou & His Famous Love Letter* (2006), XXV.

200   *Selected Correspondence of Sherman*, 707-709.

201   *Selected Correspondence of Sherman*, 600.

202   Shelby Foote, *Riot and Resurgence* (1963), 279-280. Letter from William T. Sherman to Roswell M. Sawyer dated January 1, 1863.

203   *Ibid.*

204   *Sherman's March*, 107.

205   *Ibid.*

206   William Gilmore Simms, *Sack and Destruction of the City of Columba S.C.*, 6-11.

207   Paul C. Graham, *When the Yankees Come,* 34; *See also, Voices From Slavery: 100 Authentic Slave Narratives* (2000), Norman R. Yetman, ed.

208   *See* Victor Davis Hanson, *The Soul of Battle, From Ancient Times to the Present Day, How Three Great Liberators Vanquished Tyranny* (1999).

209   Alan Dershowitz, Why Terrorism Works: Understanding the Threat, Responding to the Challenge (2002). "When I respond by describing the sterilized needle being shoved under the fingernails [torture], the reaction is visceral and often visible—a shudder coupled with a facial gesture of disgust." *Ibid.* at 141.

210   Convention Against Torture and Other Cruel, Inhuman or Degrading Treatment or Punishment, G.A. Res. 39/46, U.N. GAOR, 39th Sess., Supp. No. 51 at 198, U.N. Doc. A/39/51 (Dec. 10, 1984) [hereinafter Torture Convention].

211   *See, e.g.,* Jeffrey F. Addicott, "Into the Star Chamber: Does the United States Engage in the Use of Torture or Similar Illegal Practices in the War on Terror?," *Kentucky Law Journal* (2004), 92.

212   *Ibid.*

213   *See* Professor *Wayne* R. *LaFave.* Urbana, IL. University of Illinois College of Law. The American Law Institute, Philadelphia, PA.

214   *See* Lincoln's Gettysburg Address, December 19, 1863. Available at www.bit.ly/3WTrFnr.

215   H. W. Crocker III, *Robert E. Lee on Leadership* (1999), 67.

216   J. Karl Von Clausewitz, [J. Graham, trans.], *On War* (1918), 4.

217   *See The Sea and Beyond,* 146.

218   Thomas Robertson, "The War in Words," *Civil War Times Illustrated*, Oct. 1979, 20.

ENDNOTES

219   *When Sherman Came: Southern Women and the "Great March,"* Katharine Jones, ed., (1964), 284-286. Diary entry of March 28, 1865, from an unknown woman in Fayetteville, NC.

220   *Selected Correspondence of Sherman*, 738. Letter from Major General W. T. Sherman to Ellen Sherman (June 27, 1863).

221   *See Selected Correspondence of Sherman*, 608.

222   *To The Sea*, 65.

223   *Ibid.*, 69.

224   *Ibid.*, 61-62.

225   *See, e.g.*, Gary W. Gallagher & Joseph T. Glatthaar, *Leaders of the Lost Cause: New Perspectives on the Confederate High Command* (2004).

226   C. Joseph Bernardo & Eugene H. Bacon, *American Military Policy* (1957), 232.

227   *See* Robert C. Black III, *The Railroads of the Confederacy* (1998), 52.

228   Mark A. Weitz, *More Damning than Slaughter: Desertion in the Confederate Army* (2005), 57.

229   Donald Cartmell, *The Civil War Up Close* (2005), 26-27.

230   Martha M. Boltz, "The Civil War: "A Rich Man's Battle But a Poor Man's War," *Washington Times* (Dec. 31, 2014). Available at www. bit.ly/3vKvDmu.

231   Walter L. Fleming, *Civil War and Reconstruction in Alabama* (1905), 92.

232   OR, Ser. 3, Vol. 5, Pt. 1, p. 695.

233   Gary W. Gallagher, *The Confederate War* (1997), 28-29; James Marshall-Cornwall, *Grant* (1970), 14. Only 45 percent of the available manpower in the North was used.

234   *See* E. B. Long, *The Civil War Day by Day Almanac, 1861-1865* (1971), 710-711.

235   J. H. Segars & Charles Kelly Barrow, *Black Southerners in Confederate Armies: A Collection of Historical Accounts* (2012), 7.

236   *Ibid.*

237   Robert E. Lee, Jr., *Recollections and Letters of General Robert E. Lee* (1905), 231.

238   *See* Gary W. Gallagher, *Confederate War* (1997), 5.

239   *Ibid.*, 170. *See also* David J. Eicher, *Dixie Betrayed: How the South Really Lost the War* (2006). Eicher argues that the political infighting and failure to support Richmond by the individual States contributed to doom the South's effort to maintain its freedom.

240   *See* John M. Taylor, *Robert E. Lee and His Critics: Duty Faithfully Performed* (2000), 206-208.

241   30 *Southern Historical Society Papers* (1902), 94.

242   OR, Vol. 26, Pt. 2, p. 225.

243   See, e.g., Edward A. Miller, *Lincoln's Abolitionist General: The Biography of David Hunter* (1997).

244   *To The Sea*, 69.

245   *See* Matthew E. Winter, "Finding the Law" – The Values, Identity, and Function of the International Law Adviser," *Mil. L. Rev.* 1, 25 (1990), 128.

246   *See generally* James Lee McDonough, *William Tecumseh Sherman: In the Service of My Country* (2016).

247   *The Sea and Beyond*, xiv.

248   *See, e.g.*, Mitchell G. Klingenberg, "Sherman and His Historians: An End to the Outsized Destroyer Myth?" *Parameters (2021), 51, no. 4.*

249   *Ibid.*

250   OR, Ser. 1, Vol. 39, Pt. 2, p. 132.

251   James Lee McDonough, *William Tecumseh Sherman: In the Service of My Country* (2016), 585.

252   Justin Wintle, *The Dictionary of War Quotations* (1989), 458.

253   Clifford Dowdey, *Lee's Last Campaign* (1960), 65.

254   Jay Luvaas & Howard W. Nelson, *The U.S. Army War College Guide to the Battles of Chancellorsville and Fredericksburg* (1988), xvii; *See also* John E. Jessup Jr. & Robert W. Coakley, *A Guide to the Study and Use of Military History* (1979); Michael Shaara, *The Killer Angels* (1990). These books are just samples of many used by the United States Army in the training of its officers at Fort Leavenworth, Kansas. In addition, General Lee's Chancellorsville campaign is given detailed attention in a separate block of instruction.

255   Rev. J. Williams Jones, *Life and Letters of General Robert Edward Lee* (1906), 129.

256   Rod Gragg, The Quotable Robert E. Lee, S. Partisan, Fourth Quarter 1989, 31. Just before submitting his resignation, Lee wrote, "With all my devotion to the Union, and the feeling of loyalty and duty of an American citizen, I have not been able to make up my mind to raise my hand against my relatives, my children, and my home." *Ibid.*

257   *See* Paul C. Nagel, *The Lees of Virginia* (1990), 300-305. International recognition of Lee as a great "soldier, gentleman and Christian" first began in France, in the mid-1870's. By the first decade of the twentieth century, Britain also had become totally enthralled with Lee – in part because of the great English writer Henry James. The Canadians, who always had been sympathetic to the South, quickly expressed their

high regards for General Lee. By the time Lee died in 1870, the Montreal Telegraph was able to say, "Posterity will rank Lee above Wellington or Napoleon, before Saxe or Turenne, above Marlborough or Frederick, before Alexander, or Caesar. In fact, the greatest general of this or any other age. He made his own name, and the Confederacy he served, immortal."

258   *See* The Centennial History of the Civil War, 99.

259   *See* Gregory J.W. Urwin, *The United States Infantry* (1988),15-30. One could argue that General George Washington perhaps equaled Lee in terms of devotion shown to him by his soldiers.

260   *See* Stuart W. Smith, *Douglas Southall Freeman on Leadership* (1990). Published by the *Naval War College Press* for use in the training of senior Naval officers, it encompasses every aspect of Lee's tremendous leadership qualities. *See also* Douglas Southall Freeman, "Robert E. Lee: Maker of Morale," *Naval War College Review* (1991), 75. *See also* David Maurer, "Putting the General on the Couch," *The Daily Progress*, Sept. 30, 1991, A7. Lee's reluctance to shame or humiliate another person was probably his only handicap as a commander. Dr. J. Anderson Thomson, a noted psychiatrist from Charlottesville, Virginia, pointed out this paradox concerning Lee: "Here's a person who is considered one of the greatest leaders of men in the deadliest form of conflict known, armed warfare, who in inner-personal contacts had difficulty reprimanding or tactfully criticizing a subordinate who had disappointed or even failed him terribly." *Ibid.*

261   Rev. J. Williams Jones, *Life and Letters of General Robert Edward Lee* (1906), 128.

262   *See They Met at Gettysburg*, 25-35.

263   *Ibid.*, 28 (citing Head-Quarters Army of Northern Virginia, General Orders No. 72, dated June 21, 1863).

264   *Ibid.*, 32-34.

265   *Ibid.*, 30-31.

266   30 *Southern Historical Society Papers* (1902), 94.

267   Burke Davis, *Gray Fox* (1956), 1.

268   *See*, e.g., William J. Johnstone, *Robert E. Lee the Christian* (2013); Paul C. Nagel, *The Lees of Virginia* (1990), 301. Lee's view on Christian salvation was devoid of any form of human merit or morality although by the measure of any society, his own moral standards were impeccable. Lee understood that because God is perfect, only His plan of salvation by grace will provide salvation to sinful man. Grace oriented, he wrote, "I can only say that I am a poor sinner, trusting in Christ alone for salvation." *Ibid.*

269   *See* Charles Bracelen Flood, *Lee: The Last Years* (1981), 258-261. On October 12, 1870, Lee died of natural causes in Lexington, Virginia, where he served as the President of Washington College from 1865 to 1870. "The last distinct words that anyone heard him say were "Strike the tent!" *Ibid.*, 261.

270 *See* Rev. J. Williams Jones, *Life and Letters of General Robert Edward Lee* (1906), 482. The Cincinnati Enquirer said, "He was the great general of the 'Rebellion.' It was his strategy and superior military knowledge which kept the banner of the South afloat for so long ... ." *Ibid.*, The Philadelphia Age called him "a great master of defensive warfare ... probably not [to] be ranked inferior to any general known in history." *Ibid.*

271 *See* "General Robert E. Lee and His Famous Horse Traveler," *Confederate Veteran* 49 (1905), 13.

272 On September 14, 1814, Francis Scott Key penned "The Star-Spangled Banner," as he observed the bombardment of the American Fort McHenry at the mouth of Baltimore harbor, Maryland.

About the Author

JEFFREY F. ADDICOTT is a Professor of Law and the Director of the Warrior Defense Project at St. Mary's University School of Law, San Antonio, Texas, where he teaches a variety of courses to include National Security Law and Terrorism Law. An active duty Army officer in the Judge Advocate General's Corps for twenty years (he retired in 2000 at the rank of Lieutenant Colonel), Professor Addicott spent a quarter of his career as the senior legal advisor to the United States Army's Special Forces. An internationally recognized authority in terrorism law and the law of war, Professor Addicott not only lectures and participates in professional and academic organizations both in the United States and overseas, he is also a frequent contributor to national and international media outlets.

Foreign presentations on terrorism and national security law include numerous lectures at universities and government institutions in India, China, Sultanate of Oman, Colombia, Peru, Ukraine, Germany, France, Austria, Canada, Thailand, Japan, Honduras, Haiti, Egypt, Kuwait, Panama, Guatemala, Albania, Okinawa, Cuba, South Korea, England, Mexico, Sweden, Ireland, Scotland, Greece, Israel, Russia, and Uruguay. Presentations in the United States include over 1,000 appearances at universities and government institutions, as well as more than 5,000 appearances on radio, print, and television broadcasts to include the *Wall Street Journal, New York Times, Washington Post, Miami Herald, Dallas Star-Tribune, San Antonio Express-News, Los Angeles Times, Chicago Tribune, Washington Times, Washington Examiner,* FOX NEWS Channel, MSNBC, CNN, ABC, PBS, NBC, CBS, NPR, BBC, Voice of Russia, and al-Jazeera.

Professor Addicott is a prolific author, publishing over one hundred books, articles, and monographs on a variety of legal topics. Among his many contributions to the field, Professor Addicott pioneered the teaching of law of war and human rights courses to the militaries of numerous nascent democracies in Eastern Europe and Latin America. For these efforts he was awarded the Legion of Merit, named the "Army Judge Advocate of the Year" and honored as a co-recipient of the American Bar Association's Hodson Award.

Dr. Addicott served as the Associate Dean for Administration and Finance at St. Mary's University School of Law (2006-2007). He is also the 2007 recipient of St. Mary's University Alumni Association's "St. Mary's University School of Law Distinguished Faculty Award." Lieutenant Colonel Addicott (U.S. Army, Ret.) served in senior legal positions in Germany, Korea, Panama, and throughout the United States. Professor Addicott holds a Doctor of Juridical Science (SJD) and Master of Laws (LLM) from the University of Virginia School of Law. He also received a Master of Laws (LLM) from the Judge Advocate General's School, a Juris Doctor (JD) from the University of Alabama School of Law and a bachelor of arts with "Honors in Government" (BA) from the University of Maryland.

Latest Releases & Best Sellers

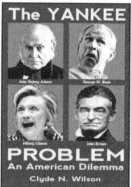

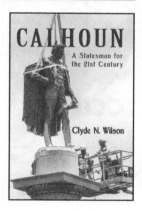
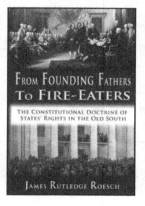
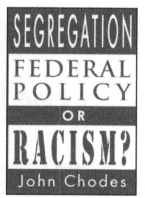

Made in United States
North Haven, CT
28 March 2024

50618520R00095